The Wealthy Gym Owner

Building a $500,000 Per Year, High-Profit Gym

Doug Spurling & Pat Rigsby

D1520546

Fitness Publishing

DOWNLOAD THE AUDIOBOOK FREE!

READ THIS FIRST!

To say thanks for purchasing our book, we would like to give you the Audiobook 100% FREE!

We know you're more likely to finish this book if you have the audiobook.

Instead of paying $10-$20 for the audiobook, we'd like to give it to you for free...

WealthyGymGift.com/Audio

VIDEO SUMMARY

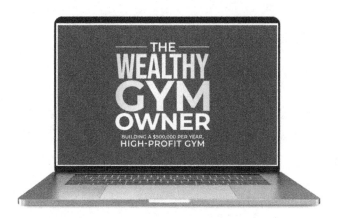

Want a video summary of this book that will help you start making progress with YOUR $500K per year gym?

Check out this video training and overview of the process.

In this training we cover 3 things:

Blueprint for $500K Growth

Proven Systems for Scale

Build Wealth Beyond the Gym

WealthyGymGift.com/Video

Want Our Help at
WealthyGymOwners.com?

Want our help implementing the strategies in The Wealthy Gym Owner?

We'll guide you step-by-step to:

- **Shift From Trainer to CEO** – Learn to delegate, lead, and work on your business, not in it.
- **Master Profitable Systems** – From marketing automation to financial frameworks like "Profit First."
- **Drive Retention & Growth** – Build client experiences that keep members loyal and turn them into raving fans.
- **Create a Wealth-Building Game Plan** – Leverage your gym to fund real estate, new locations, or other income streams.

At WealthyGymOwners.com, we'll save you hundreds of hours and thousands of dollars while helping you scale a profitable, thriving gym business.

If you're ready to fast-track your success and implement these proven strategies, book a free call with us today. Together, we'll create a personalized plan to help you hit your goals:

WealthyGymGift.com/Apply

Wealthy Gym Owner: Building a $500,000 Per Year, High-Profit Gym

Disclaimer

This book is intended to provide information and tools to help you start and grow a gym business. However, the author makes no guarantees regarding the outcomes of implementing the advice or strategies outlined in this book. Success in business is influenced by numerous factors beyond the author's control, including market conditions, individual effort, and local regulations. Therefore, readers should use their discretion and seek additional professional guidance as necessary.

First Edition

ISBN: 9798306912318

Printed in United States

Table of Contents

Introduction

If you're reading this, chances are you're a gym owner—or dreaming of becoming one—who wants to make an impact and a profit. You're driven, maybe even passionate, about fitness, and you've got big goals. But let's face it, having big goals alone won't turn a gym into a high-profit business. This book is here to bridge that gap, to provide a roadmap that helps you move from passion to profitability.

Building a gym that pulls in $500,000 a year is no small feat. It's a mix of hard work, smart strategies, and avoiding the pitfalls that swallow up so many well-intentioned gym owners. Too often, entrepreneurs enter this industry with nothing more than a love of fitness, a few clients, and a rented space, only to struggle with cash flow, client retention, and burnout. They pour their time and energy into training sessions, hoping that their passion alone will fuel growth. But without a clear vision and solid business structure, they soon find themselves spinning their wheels.

Most books on gym ownership or business strategies focus on either the technical side of training or the basics of running a business. But few focus on how to scale a gym specifically into a high-revenue, high-impact business... one where systems are streamlined, client experiences are top-notch, and profitability isn't an afterthought. This book is designed to fill that gap. It's not about offering generic business advice but giving gym owners a precise guide to building a gym that thrives financially and grows sustainably.

Our own experience in the fitness business is hard-earned. We've been on both sides of the story: the trainer who was all about results and the business owner who had to learn how to build a profitable gym from the ground up. We've both walked this path, seen the highs and lows, and learned what it takes to build a gym that isn't just another business, but a thriving community that makes a difference.

This journey isn't theoretical for us... *it's practical, tested, and effective.*

Building a $500,000 gym requires more than just passion for fitness. It takes a blend of strategic vision, strong leadership, and smart financial management. In this book, we're going to walk you through the strategies that helped us and thousands of clients we've collectively served...turn a small, dream-driven operation into a high-profit business. You'll learn how to build a powerful brand, create client-centered systems, and grow your revenue consistently, without losing sight of why you started this journey in the first place.

If you're ready to step up as a business owner, this book is your blueprint. It's not just for the coaches or the dreamers, it's for those who are serious about building a thriving gym business. This book will guide you around the pitfalls, teach you the systems, and provide the roadmap to turn your vision into a profitable reality. Let's get started on creating the gym you've envisioned—one that's both rewarding to run and financially successful.

PART I

Become the Owner

Master More Than Training

Chapter 1

Build Your Business Around a Clear Vision

The Importance of Vision and Goals for Building a $500,000 per Year Gym

If you want to build a $500,000 per year gym, you need more than just passion - you need a clear vision and well-defined goals.

It's easy to get caught up in the day-to-day grind and if you don't know exactly where you're headed, you'll struggle to get there.

Having a strong vision gives you direction, while clear goals provide the roadmap for getting there. The reason we want to have a solid vision is that it forms the bedrock for and informs how you develop solid systems, marketing plans, and financial goals.

Start with a Clear Vision

Your vision is your long-term destination. It's what you want your gym to look like, feel like, and accomplish. Having a crystal-clear vision helps guide every decision you make in your business.

Do you want to build a gym focused on high-end, 1 on 1 personal training?

Or perhaps a small group training model?

Whatever your vision is, it needs to be specific and meaningful to you. It's what keeps you motivated when things get tough and provides a framework for your long-term strategy.

Your vision should be big. If your goal is $500,000 (or more) per year, ask yourself what that looks like.

How many clients do you need?

What kind of services will you offer?

What kind of culture will you build?

The clearer your vision, the easier it will be to map out the steps to achieve it.

Break Down Your Vision into Goals

Once you have your vision, you need to break it down into actionable goals.

Goals are the stepping stones that take you from where you are now to where you want to be. Having measurable, time-bound goals is crucial for tracking your progress and making adjustments along the way.

For a $500,000 per year gym, start by determining your key metrics.

How much revenue do you need each month?

How many clients at what price point will help you hit those numbers?

Then, break it down further. If you need 100 clients paying $400 per month, how many new clients do you need to bring in each month?

How will you retain the ones you already have?

These goals should be specific, measurable, and aligned with your vision.

Stay Focused and Review Regularly

Consistency is key. You need to regularly review your goals to see what's working and what isn't. If something isn't moving you toward your $500,000 goal, adjust and try something else.

Vision and goals aren't just a one-time exercise, they're ongoing.

Every few months, revisit your goals, track your progress, and make sure they still align with your overall vision.

Remember, building a $500,000 (or more) per year gym is absolutely achievable, but only if you have a clear vision and goals to guide you. Your vision gives you direction, and your goals break the journey into manageable steps. With the right focus and a commitment to regular review, you'll be well on your way to hitting or exceeding that half-million mark.

Key Takeaways:

1. ***Define Success Clearly****: Craft a vision for what your $500,000 gym looks like, including your client base, services, and culture. Without clarity, it's easy to lose focus in the daily grind.*

2. ***Turn Vision into Goals****: Break down your vision into specific, measurable, and time-bound goals. Each goal should directly connect to your big-picture success plan.*

3. ***Consistently Evaluate Progress****: Regularly review your goals to ensure alignment with your vision. Adjust when necessary to stay on track.*

Chapter 2

The Transition from Trainer to Business Owner

Moving from being a trainer to becoming a business owner is a big leap. It's exciting, but let's be honest... it's a lot to handle. You're not just focused on delivering great workouts anymore. You're managing operations, marketing, finances, and a team. The skills that made you a great trainer won't be enough alone. To succeed, you need to start thinking like an entrepreneur. But here's the good news: with the right mindset and strategies, you can build a thriving business.

Shift from Trainer to Owner

The first big challenge in this transition is changing how you think. As a trainer, you've always been focused on your clients... making sure they hit their goals and giving them the best experience possible. But now, you need to step back and look at the bigger picture. You're not just responsible for each client's success, you're responsible for the success of your entire business.

This is where the shift to thinking like a business owner comes in. It's crucial to move from the mindset of a coach to that of a CEO. You have to start looking at your business like an entrepreneur - planning for growth, managing people, and focusing on the long-term vision.

You need to step up as a leader and embrace the role of CEO. As your gym grows, your role must evolve. And this involves: You need to delegate, build a team, and create a culture that reflects your vision. Strong leadership is crucial for guiding your team and ensuring everyone is working toward the same goals.

Build Systems for Consistency

One of the biggest differences between being a trainer and being a business owner is the need to create systems that work for your team.

Why are systems important? Because, you don't have the time or ability to do all the jobs required for your business to run smoothly. And you also don't have the time to train every individual on the way that you want things done.

So, what you need to do is create 'systems' - or thought out, efficient guides for completing tasks that every employee can follow. Systems are the backbone of a scalable business. They help create consistency and ensure that your business runs smoothly even when you're not there. You need systems for onboarding clients, managing staff, and keeping your marketing machine running. And there are so many more categories of the business that you'll need to map out with a system.

Systems that Scale

One of the most important aspects of building a $500K gym is creating scalable systems. Systems are the backbone of a successful fitness business.

From onboarding clients to managing finances, everything needs a system. These systems ensure consistency, reduce errors, and allow you to scale without sacrificing quality.

For example, your client onboarding system should be seamless, ensuring every new member feels welcome and understands your gym's culture.

A marketing system that regularly generates leads and keeps your pipeline full is also essential.

The key here is to create repeatable processes so your gym can grow without you needing to handle every detail yourself.

By creating systems, you'll free up your time and energy to focus on growing the business rather than putting out fires every day.

Learn to Delegate and Build a Team

Most trainers struggle with delegation. As a trainer, you're used to being hands-on with everything.

You run your sessions, manage your client relationships, and control all aspects of the service. But as a business owner, you need to let go of some of that control.

You can't do it all. To grow, you need to step back and trust your trainers to deliver the same level of service that your clients expect from you. That means investing in their development and training them to align with your vision.

But it's not just about your trainers.

You'll also need help with other aspects of the business, like marketing, sales, and administration. Hiring the right people to handle these tasks allows you to focus on the bigger picture and keep the business growing.

Focus on Retention, Not Just New Clients

Most new business owners focus heavily on getting clients through the door. That's important, but keeping the clients you already have is what truly drives growth.

Retention is key. A client who stays with you for years is much more valuable than one who leaves after a few months. Why is retention so important? It's because it costs much more to attract a new client than to keep a current one. As a bonus, happy clients bring in new clients through referrals. Make it easy for your clients to refer friends, and reward them when they do. It's a win-win situation.

To improve retention, you need systems that keep clients engaged. That could mean regular check-ins, personalized programs, or special events that build community.

Pricing for Profitability

Another key element in building a $500K gym is pricing your services correctly. You can't compete on price alone, especially when there are bigger, more well-funded competitors in your area.

Instead, focus on the results your clients will get and the unique experience you offer.

Focus on Retention

Bringing in new clients is essential, but retaining them is what will keep your gym profitable. The cost of acquiring a new client is much higher than keeping an existing one.

To keep clients coming back, you need to create a community where they feel supported and motivated.

Regular check-ins, progress tracking, and member appreciation events all help build loyalty.

Plus, focusing on your client relationships creates opportunities for upselling and referrals.

Focus on delivering value to your clients, retaining them, and consistently improving your operations.

Master the Business Fundamentals

Here's something trainers who become owners of their own gym often overlook: the need to dive deeply into learning about the fundamentals of running a business. Being great at fitness and coaching isn't enough anymore. You need to know how to run the *'back-end'* of your gym.

What do I mean by 'back-end?'

1. You need to understand your finances. In order to run a successful gym, you need to know what money is coming in, what is going out, what services are popular, and why. Ideally, before even starting your business you would have sat down with your trusted financial expert and created a budget to track your key metrics like client *acquisition costs, profit margins, and lifetime client value. These values will need to be updated regularly so that you know the up to date financial health of your business.* Knowing your numbers allows you to make smarter decisions and avoid common pitfalls.

Financial Mastery - You can't build a $500K gym without mastering your finances.

Tracking key financial metrics - like client acquisition cost, profit margins, and average revenue per member - will give you a clear picture of your gym's health.

Regularly review your pricing, expenses, and profitability to make sure you're on track.

2. You need a structured marketing plan. Your reputation might have kept you busy as a trainer, running a business requires a more structured marketing plan. This means creating a monthly marketing system, using social proof (like client success stories), and running referral campaigns that keep new leads coming in.

A Strong Marketing Machine

To build a $500K gym, you need to master marketing. A consistent marketing strategy is essential. You can't rely on word-of-mouth alone...you need a plan that includes online lead generation, referral programs, and local marketing.

Start by developing a monthly marketing calendar that covers lead generation, client engagement, and referral campaigns.

This ensures that you're not scrambling at the last minute to bring in new business.

Automating parts of your marketing will also help keep things running smoothly while you focus on the big picture.

And don't forget about referral marketing. Make it easy for your clients to refer their friends and reward them when they do.

Creating a strong referral culture is one of the best ways to grow your client base consistently.

Stay Focused on Growth

It's easy to get bogged down in the day-to-day operations when you're running a gym.

But if you want to succeed as a business owner, you need to keep your eyes on the future. That means setting goals, regularly reviewing your progress, and constantly improving the way that you do things.

Whether it's refining your onboarding process, improving your sales strategy, or creating new upsell opportunities, you should always be looking for ways to grow.

The transition from trainer to business owner isn't easy, but it's one of the most rewarding moves you can make in your career.

It requires a shift in mindset, a focus on systems, the ability to build and lead a team using delegation skills, and a disciplined study of business fundamentals. These are the stepping stones required to build a sustainable and profitable gym.

Key Takeaways:

1. ***Think Like a CEO****: Shift your focus from daily tasks to long-term strategy. Build systems and delegate so you can lead, not just manage.*

2. ***Build Scalable Systems****: Create repeatable processes for marketing, onboarding, and retention. Systems ensure consistency and free your time to grow the business.*

3. ***Invest in Delegation****: Develop your team's skills so they can execute your vision. Let go of control and empower others to thrive.*

PART II

Connect

Position Your Gym

Chapter 3

Establish Your Brand Identity

Making Your Gym Magnetic

Have you ever done a Google search of all the gyms in your area? Take a second and do that now. How many came up on Google maps? Five? Ten? Twenty? Maybe more? Depending on where your business is located [urban, suburban or rural], you might have some heavy competition. So, how do you stand out from the other gyms in your area?

The answer is pretty simple: Be different. Establish a visual reminder of who you are and what you want to be known for. That is essentially what is behind a brand identity. And you need to get this right.

Establish a strong brand identity.

How, you ask? First, I want to tell you exactly what a brand identity is and isn't. It's not just about your logo or the colors on your website. Your brand is much more than that. It's the promise you make to your clients and how they feel every time they interact with you.

Creating a brand that resonates with your audience and keeps them coming back is key to building a successful training business.

And here's the good news: you don't need a massive budget to do it.

What you need is clarity, consistency, and the right story.

Clarity is Key

The first step in building your brand is clarity. If people are confused about what you offer, they'll keep looking. Think of your messaging like a conversation with a potential client... they need to know exactly what you do and why it matters to them.

Ask yourself:

- Can someone describe my brand in one sentence?

- Is it clear what I offer and how it benefits my ideal clients?

If your message is too complicated or full of jargon, potential clients will tune out. You need to be crystal clear about how you solve their problems, whether that's helping them lose weight, perform better, or feel more confident in themselves.

So, refine your messaging until anyone can understand it at a glance.

Your Brand is Not the Hero

Here's something a lot of business owners get wrong: Your brand isn't the hero. Your client is the hero. Your brand is the guide.

Think of it like this: In any good story, the hero is on a journey, and the guide helps them get where they want to go.

In *"Star Wars,"* Luke Skywalker is the hero. Yoda is the guide.

Your clients are Luke. You are Yoda.

So instead of making your marketing all about you...your qualifications, your experience...focus on your client's journey. How will you help them succeed? How will your program change their life? When you shift the focus from you to them, you'll see a much stronger connection with your prospects.

Consistency Builds Trust

Branding isn't just about having a good message... it's about delivering that message consistently. People trust brands that deliver the same experience time and time again.

Whether it's how you show up on social media or how you are in person...be consistent.

If you promise a welcoming, supportive community, but your gym feels cold or uninviting, prospects will feel that disconnect. Your brand needs to be consistent across every touchpoint...whether it's online or in-person. Your clients should feel like they know what to expect from you, every time.

Storytelling is Powerful

Let's talk about storytelling. People don't just buy products or services, they buy into the story behind those products. Let me give you an example.

A while back, there was a clothing retailer, The J. Peterman Company, that sold stories.

When people discovered the J. Peterman Company, it felt like stepping into a movie set. Each item—from rugged leather jackets to well-worn fedoras—came with a story, like the City Slicker's Coat or The Hemingway Shirt.

But people weren't just buying a shirt; they were buying the feeling of adventure. Wearing it, they felt transformed, as if they'd just stepped off a plane in some faraway place, ready for anything.

And your brand is no different.

Your clients are on a journey, and your brand should help guide them toward their goals.

So, how do you tell a compelling story?

1. **Define the problem**: What challenges are your clients facing? Maybe they've tried other gyms and didn't see results. Maybe they're struggling to stay motivated. Whatever it is, identify their pain points.

2. **Be the guide**: Show that you have the expertise and ability to help them overcome their challenges. Share testimonials or success stories that show how others like them have succeeded with your help.

3. **Call to action**: Don't be shy about asking for the next step. Whether it's a free trial or a paid program, make sure your message includes a clear call to action.

When your prospective clients see that they are dealing with the same problem you mention in your story, and that what you offer might help them, they're more likely to connect with your brand on an emotional level.

Build an Emotional Connection

At the end of the day, people make decisions based on emotion. Sure, logic plays a role, but emotions drive action.

If you can tap into the emotions your clients feel, whether it's the frustration of not seeing results or the excitement of becoming a better version of themselves, you'll build a stronger connection.

Use stories, visuals, and language that evoke the emotions your clients want to feel.

Show before-and-after photos, share client transformations, or post motivational content that inspires them to take action. When your brand makes people feel something, they'll keep coming back.

Stand Out by Being Unique

The industry is crowded. So, how do you stand out?

Differentiate yourself.

What makes your gym or program unique? Maybe it's your personalized approach, your focus on a specific target market, or the tight-knit community you've built. Whatever it is, make sure it's clear in your branding.And be specific. When people know what makes you different, they'll know why they should choose you over the competition.

What if my services aren't different?

Remember, your brand isn't just about what you offer, it's about how you make people feel. When you position your clients as the hero of the story and show that you're the guide who can help them succeed, you'll build a brand that stands out in a crowded market.

Key Takeaways:

1. ***Clarity Wins***: *Your brand should communicate who you are and how you help clients. Simplify your messaging so anyone can understand it in seconds.*

2. ***Clients Are the Hero***: *Position your clients' transformation as the focus of your marketing. You're the guide helping them achieve their goals.*

3. ***Consistency Builds Trust***: *Deliver a seamless and predictable experience across all touchpoints—from social media to your gym floor.*

Chapter 4

Target the Perfect Prospect

The Key to Growing Your Gym

So, let's say that you've created your vision, and you have your brand story all laid out. But you still don't get much business, especially not new customers. You wonder why. When I encounter clients who are facing difficulties like this at the beginning of their gym ownership journey, it is often for one of these two reasons: They're casting too wide of a net, trying to appeal to everyone. Or, they're pursuing people that don't need them.

And this is a result of something called improper prospect targeting. A fancy way of saying, you're not telling your story to the right people.

When I ask any gym owner about growing their business, the topic of targeting the right prospects comes up. Invariably, I ask them to...

"...Tell me about your perfect prospect."

And while they often implied that they know their audience inside and out, most of them come up pretty short when I ask for the details about who they want to serve.

If you want to grow your gym the right way, you've got to focus on the perfect prospect... the people who not only fit your gym but are also the most likely to stay, refer friends, and become long-term clients.

Here's how you do it:

Know Who You Want to Work With

First things first: *who do you really want to work with?* If your answer is "everyone," you're already missing the point.

Successful gyms don't try to cater to everyone. They focus on a specific group of people that aligns with their vision, culture, strengths, and services. First, review your vision again. Read it out loud to yourself.

Take a moment to picture your ideal client.

What do they look like?

How old are they?

What's important to them?

What do they think about training?

What have they tried in the past?

Now...look back to who they were when they initially came in contact with you and your gym.

What changed about them?

That's a good starting point.

Define Their Pain Points

Once you've got a general idea of who you want to work with, dig a little deeper. What problems or challenges are they facing? Are they struggling to stay consistent with their workouts? Do they feel intimidated by other gyms? Maybe they're overwhelmed and don't know where to start.

Understanding their pain points is key to positioning your gym as the solution they've been looking for. Think about it—your perfect prospects might:

- Not feel they have time to work out.

- Feel too intimidated to walk into a typical training gym.

- Need accountability and can't find it anywhere else.

Once you know their struggles, you can show them how your gym solves those problems. The clearer you can articulate their pain points... and the solutions your gym offers...the more likely they'll see your gym as the perfect fit.

Craft Messaging That Speaks to Them

Most gyms drop the ball when it comes to messaging, creating generic taglines that mean little to nothing to their perfect prospects.

Or they throw up ads that try to appeal to everyone...but the reality is that they often strongly appeal to no one.

Those ads get lost in the noise.

Your messaging needs to be personal. When your ideal client sees your ad, visits your website or sees anything representing you online, they should feel like you're talking directly to them or that what they're seeing of you is attractive.

Here's how you create messaging that works:

- **Speak their language**: Use the same words and phrases your perfect prospect uses. If you're targeting busy professionals, talk about quick, results-driven workouts that fit their schedule. If you're targeting parents, emphasize flexibility and convenience.

- **Address their pain points**: Focus on solving their specific problems. If consistency is an issue, highlight your accountability systems. If intimidation is a concern, talk about how supportive your gym environment is.

- **Paint a picture of success**: Show them what their life could look like after they join your gym. Use actual client examples. Make it clear that you understand their struggles and that your gym is the solution they've been waiting for.

Go Where Your Perfect Prospect Already Is

If you want to reach your perfect prospect, you need to *be where they are.* Too many gym owners rely on organic posts or basic ads that cast a wide net, hoping the right people will find them. But that's not enough. You need to be more strategic. Ask your best clients: What do they read, watch, or listen to? What businesses do they frequent? Once you know, you can tailor your marketing efforts to meet them where they are.

Here's how:

- **Social media targeting**: Use Facebook and Instagram ads to target your audience based on their interests and behaviors.

- **Local partnerships**: Team up with businesses your perfect prospect frequents. If you're targeting parents, partner with local schools or daycares. For professionals, do lunch & learns.

- **Community events**: Sponsor events that your perfect prospect attends. If you're targeting weekend warriors, sponsor a local race. If you're targeting parents, set up a booth at school or sports events.

By going where your perfect prospect is, you're not just hoping they'll find you...you're actively positioning your gym as their perfect solution.

Focus on Value, Not Just Features

Here's a big mistake many owners make: they focus on features, not value.

People don't become clients because of your class schedule or equipment. They buy into your brand because they want the results that come from using those things.

When you're marketing to your perfect prospect, focus on the value you provide. What transformation can they expect?

When you focus on value, you show your perfect prospect how your gym can change their life... not just give them a place to work out.

Build Long-Term Relationships

Here's the final step... once your perfect prospect walks through your doors, you need to make sure they stay.

The key is building long-term relationships.

Here's how:

- **Deliver exceptional service**: From day one, show them that they've made the right choice.

- **Provide personalized attention**: Whether it's check-ins or accountability calls, make sure they feel supported.

- **Foster a sense of community**: Encourage them to connect with other clients and celebrate their milestones.

When you focus on building relationships, you're not just attracting members - you're creating loyal clients who stay for the long haul.

Key Takeaways:

1. *Identify Your Ideal Client: Stop trying to serve everyone—focus on the people who truly align with your gym's mission and culture. The clearer your target, the stronger your messaging will be.*

2. *Solve Their Problems: Understand the pain points your ideal clients face, such as intimidation, time constraints, or lack of accountability, and show how your gym is the solution.*

Meet Them Where They Are: *Be strategic about reaching prospects by targeting the places they frequent—partner with local businesses, use targeted social media ads, and engage in community events.*

Chapter 5

The Role of Content Marketing in Building Authority

In today's world, most business models aren't going to do well if they don't incorporate digital marketing strategies, particularly content marketing. When done right, content marketing helps position your gym as a trusted expert in the fitness industry while creating meaningful connections with your audience. It's about sharing valuable, relevant information that resonates with your prospects and clients, keeping your gym top-of-mind when they're ready to make decisions about their health and fitness.

So, how can you unleash your expertise onto your digital audience in a meaningful and impactful way? Before we answer that question, we have to nail out a few terms.

Organic marketing refers to any marketing strategy that doesn't require direct payment to distribute content. This includes social media posts, blog articles, SEO, email newsletters, and word-of-mouth. Organic marketing is essential for building long-term trust with your audience.

This is especially true for gyms, where your reputation, the results you deliver, and your community are key selling points.

Pros of Organic Marketing

Cost-Effective: Organic marketing doesn't require direct payment, making it budget-friendly for new or smaller gyms.

Builds Authority and Trust: When you consistently provide value, whether through social media tips, blog content, or client testimonials...you position your gym as an authority. Over time, this builds credibility and trust.

Improves Visibility: Regularly posting relevant content improves your gym's visibility, making it easier for new clients to find you.

Cons of Organic Marketing: Takes Time: Organic marketing is a long game. It takes time to build an audience, rank on search engines, and turn followers into clients.

Limited Reach: Social media platforms limit the reach of organic posts, so it may take longer to gain visibility. You're relying on algorithms and word-of-mouth, which can be slow to scale.

Paid Marketing: Accelerating Growth:

Paid marketing involves paying for exposure, typically through platforms like Facebook Ads, Instagram Ads and Google Ads. Paid marketing can help you accelerate your lead generation efforts by targeting the right audience with specific offers.

Pros of Paid Marketing:

1. **Immediate Results:** Unlike organic marketing, paid ads can bring in leads quickly. With the right targeting, you can have new prospects inquiring about your services within hours or days.

2. **Control Over Audience:** Paid ads allow you to precisely target the demographics you want... based on location, age, interests, and even behaviors. This means you're spending money to reach your ideal prospect.

3. **Scalability:** Paid marketing can be scaled as needed. If an ad campaign is performing well, you can easily increase the budget to reach more people and generate more leads.

Cons of Paid Marketing:

1. **It Can Get Expensive:** Paid marketing requires an investment. If not managed correctly, it can quickly become expensive without yielding significant results.

2. **Visibility is Short-Term:** Once you stop paying for ads, your visibility disappears. Unlike organic marketing, which continues to deliver results over time, paid marketing only works as long as you're actively spending money.

Combining Organic and Paid Marketing

The best strategy is often a combination of both approaches. Organic marketing helps build your brand's reputation and trust over time, while paid marketing can bring in immediate leads and accelerate growth.

By balancing the two, you can ensure steady, sustainable growth. Use organic content to engage and nurture your audience, then amplify successful campaigns or promotions with targeted paid ads. Organic marketing provides long-term stability and brand trust, while paid marketing gives you the speed and reach needed to grow quickly.

Both are important tools for scaling your gym effectively.

Now that you understand the two most common types of digital marketing, we are going to move on to give you tips on how to build your audience and keep them engaged through an authoritative presence and a consistent content marketing strategy..

Educating Your Audience

One of the primary goals of content marketing is to educate your audience. By consistently sharing informative content that helps people solve their fitness problems, you demonstrate expertise – eventually becoming your prospect's go-to expert. When you offer insights that people find helpful, they begin to trust you. And trust is a crucial component of authority. Whether it's a post explaining the benefits of different training methods or a guide on how to recover after a workout, your audience will view you as a reliable source of knowledge.

Building a Relationship with Your Audience

Content marketing is not just about sharing information, it's also about building relationships.

Through regular, consistent content, you can engage with your audience on a deeper level. Platforms like social media and email newsletters allow you to connect with your clients and prospects, offering them continuous value even when they're not at your gym. By doing this, you create an ongoing conversation with your audience, keeping your gym relevant in their minds.

Showcasing Social Proof

Another critical way content marketing helps build authority is through social proof. In our industry, showcasing client success stories, transformations, and testimonials is a great way to prove that your methods work. Regularly sharing client wins can help potential clients trust your gym's ability to deliver results. By highlighting real-world success stories, you demonstrate that you don't just talk the talk, you walk the walk. This kind of content validates your expertise and makes your gym more attractive to new clients.

Establishing Long-Term Authority

Unlike paid ads, which stop generating leads once the budget runs out, content marketing continues to work long after it's published. Videos and social media content are somewhat evergreen, providing long-term value and continually attracting new prospects over time. This long-lasting impact helps establish your gym's authority in a sustainable way, giving you a steady flow of leads and helping your reputation grow organically. Content marketing isn't just about promoting your gym for today, it's about building trust, educating your audience, and demonstrating your expertise. By consistently delivering value through high-quality content, you can position your gym as the authority in your area, driving new leads, new clients, and long-term retention. When it comes to marketing your gym, you'll often hear two main strategies mentioned: organic marketing and paid marketing.

Both play valuable roles in growing your business, but understanding how they work and when to use each one is the key to getting the best results.

Let's break down the pros and cons of both approaches so you can decide which one makes the most sense for your gym.

Key Takeaways:

1. **Educate to Dominate**: *Share content that helps your audience solve problems, like fitness tips or recovery guides. Become the go-to expert by consistently delivering value.*

2. **Leverage Social Proof**: *Highlight client testimonials, transformations, and reviews to build trust. People trust real stories and results.*

Blend Organic and Paid Marketing: *Use organic content to build trust and authority, then amplify your reach with targeted paid ads to drive immediate results.*

Chapter 6

Fill Your Gym

Winning Strategies for Lead Generation

When it comes to growing your gym, lead generation is key. Without a steady flow of new leads, it's hard to scale your business or replace clients who churn. But the goal isn't just about capturing as many leads as possible... it's about attracting high-quality leads who are the right fit for your gym. You need a sustainable strategy that generates consistent results and converts those leads into long-term members.

Here's how to build a lead generation machine that works for your gym.

Create Value-Driven, Congruent Lead Magnets

A lead magnet is a valuable resource you can offer in exchange for a prospect's contact information.

Your lead magnet should be congruent with the services you provide. This way, you attract leads who are genuinely interested in what you have to offer.

Once you've created your lead magnet, promote it through your website, social media, and email marketing... and, ultimately, with paid ads. Make sure it offers enough value that prospects are willing to exchange their contact details, giving you the chance to nurture and convert them over time.

Utilize Referral Marketing

Referral marketing is a great way to use your current clients to draw in more business. This is where you ask your current clients to refer their family or friends to come in and try out your business. It is often not done enough, or not done well enough to grow your business.If done well, however, your growth could be only limited by your own imagination. Referrals, in my opinion, should be your preferred method to getting more business.

You already have a captured audience, who continues to stay with your business because you've helped them achieve some goal. And referrals happen because your current clients believe that you can help someone they know—a family member, a friend, or even a co-worker—reach their own personal goals.

You, as a business owner, should be leveraging your clients to make the connection. And to make this happen, you can offer incentives so they are rewarded for their efforts. These incentives could keep them referring their family and friends to you month after month. If your referral program is done correctly, you should expect each client that comes to visit your facility or studio, or refer at least 1 person each month. Even if they don't sign up, you have now formed a relationship with that person, so they may join or hire you in the future, or when the time is right.

Why Is Referral Marketing So Important?

Besides being the number one way to drive in more business, referral marketing is a great way to attract the people you want to target... it can also yield the longest, more tenured clients in your facility. These are the people that love what you do, have had tremendous success with your business, and are more than willing to spread the word of what your services can do for them. Referral marketing is both efficient, and effective, at bringing new leads into your facility.

And the best part: You can get a lot of leads without leaving your facility. This is great because you can spend more time doing what you love, and not chasing down new leads that could benefit from your service.

By focusing your business as the *"top referral business around,"* it again leads to more quality leads coming through your door, and less time following up before you convert them into a paying client.

How To Include Referral Marketing Into Your Business

Besides coming out and asking your clients for a referral, there are plenty of tactics you can implement that will encourage them to spread the word about your services.

Some of these tactics include:

Point-of-Sale Gift Card

This occurs when someone first signs up for your services. You offer them a gift card so they can pass it on to a family member, or friend, who may benefit from your services. It could be a free month membership, or a two-week trial to a class or training. This drives in new traffic, as they are excited to bring in a friend or family member to workout with them.

Point-of-Sale Friend Request

As part of your membership packet, you can include a friend request form—where they give you a few names, and the contact information of their friends, so you can contact them and invite them to try a class on the house. Although a little bit tougher to ask for a few names, this can give you the opportunity to reach out to them yourself, and invite them in to give your business a try. You can offer them a free class or a free screening just for coming in. During this time, you can get more information from them, and show them how you can help them reach their goals.

Bring-a-Friend Event

This is where you hold a class, or event, that allows your current clients to bring in a friend for free. This gives the potential client a chance to see if this is something that will benefit them, and if it's worth their time. It also allows a new member to feel comfortable since they are able to exercise with someone they are close to.

Charity Events

A charity event is a great way to raise awareness for a particular charity and gives your business plenty of exposure. This allows you to run a class where all the proceeds go to a charity of your choice. Not only does this allow someone to do their part and give to a good cause, it gives you the chance to show them what you can do to help them reach their goals. It also adds another strategic partnership to your business that could be a great referral source.

Ask For Advice

This is another event that allows your current clients to bring in a friend or family member that may have initial questions about your services. It gives them a chance to get their questions answered, without the pressure of having to sign up right away. It also provides you the chance to share your knowledge, and sell your potential customer on what you can do for them.

Guest Invitation Drives

These quarterly or semi-annual drives are events geared at getting new people to walk through your doors and check out what you have to offer. This is the perfect time to get your current clients to refer their friends, and offer incentives to them if they are successful at referring someone to you. During this type drive, you can hold drawings, raffles, or other fun activities to get more people excited about your business.

Referral Contests

This type of contest is for those who are very competitive. You can offer prizes for the top referrers, or give different prizes for reaching different referral levels. For example, if someone brings in 5 new members, they get a discounted rate on membership, or training services.

Challenge/Program Gift

This goes along with the referral contest. You can also offer everyone who refers someone to your business, a free gift as a thank you for participating.

Leverage Local Marketing Partnerships

Local marketing is often overlooked, but it's an effective way to tap into your community's network. Even though people may spend a lot of time online, it's not the only place they look for information. Many of your potential clients spend a lot of time "offline" or in their local communities. Although there are many different forms of 'local' marketing, some of the more popular ones include:

Organic Networking

The idea of networking should be one of the first offline strategies you should work on. Organic networking works by creating connections, and building relationships with your clients. It also provides a more natural way to get to know people, what they may need and want, and how you can help them because you are sharing something in common.

Structured Networking

This is slightly different from organic networking. This is a more formal, meeting-style of networking that offers personal introductions at conferences and meetings. It helps your potential client have a more productive time because they are introduced to the right person who may help them reach their goals faster.

Public Speaking

Public speaking is by far one of the best, and most effective ways, to get your message in front of the right people. So it's time to dust off your shoes and book some more speaking gigs. This is the perfect way to share your knowledge, and sell your potential client on your business being the solution to their problem. You can speak at libraries, churches, lunch-and-learns, conferences... or really anywhere that people tend to meet and share information. This builds a relationship with your clients, so they are more comfortable with you, and your business. They may be more comfortable reaching out to you, and seeing how you can help them reach their goals.

Strategic Partnerships

Strategic partnerships are when you connect with local businesses that cater to your potential customer. It could be physical therapy offices, chiropractors, doctor's offices, hair salons, and massage therapists. This creates a beneficial relationship between both businesses so you can both refer clients back and forth to each respective business.

Direct Mail

Although this may be pricey to do, direct mail, next to door-to-door selling, is one of the most effective marketing methods to get your message in front of as many people as possible. You can buy a list from a local brokering business, with the sole purpose of sending a piece of direct mail explaining your services. But remember, people have a short attention span. The message needs to highlight their pain to get them reading and then needs to provide the solution they're looking for.

To create the most enticing offer—and get them to contact you—you need to follow this template:

- Have a headline that appeals to their specific needs.

- The lead is one of the most important parts of any letter. You need to emotionally hook them (possibly with a good story), or show that you understand their pain points.

- Address their pain points and agitate them.

- Show them how you are the solution to their problems—and what you can offer them.

- Have a strong CTA (call to action) to get them to take action.

Before online marketing was popular, direct mail was the preferred choice for getting a company's message in front of the right audience.

Featured Business or Organization

After you've forged your strategic partnerships, you can start to use a *"featured business or organization"* campaign. This is where you highlight one of the businesses you're connected with, and you offer their clients a special promotion.It could be a free workshop, a free screen, or some other service they can take advantage of. You can also give the employees of the business a discount to train with you, which could give their clients more of an incentive to also work with you. Featured business marketing can build loyalty, which could lead to more referrals for your business.

Use Social Proof to Build Trust

When it comes to lead generation, nothing builds trust faster than social proof. People want to see that your gym produces real results. Consistently sharing member success stories is essential for attracting new leads.

Here's how to leverage social proof:

- **Share Success Stories**: Post before-and-after photos, testimonials, and client success stories on your social media, website, and newsletters. These real-life examples show potential clients the transformation your gym can deliver.

- **Encourage Google Reviews**: Ask your current members to leave reviews on platforms like Google, Yelp, or Facebook. Positive reviews not only boost your credibility but also improve your gym's search rankings, making it easier for new leads to find you.

- **Video Testimonials**: Short video testimonials from satisfied clients can be especially powerful. Video feels more authentic and personal, which helps prospects connect with your brand.

Implement Targeted Paid Advertising

While organic growth is critical, targeted paid advertising can accelerate your lead generation efforts. Platforms like Facebook and Instagram allow you to target your ideal clients based on location, interests, and demographics. Here's how to make the most of paid advertising:

- **Geo-Targeting**: Use geo-targeting to ensure your ads are seen by people within your gym's local radius. This increases the likelihood of attracting leads who are close enough to attend.

- **Highlight Special Offers**: Promote limited-time offers, like a free trial or discounted membership, to drive urgency and action.

- **Retarget Visitors**: Set up retargeting ads to reach people who've already visited your website but haven't signed up. These ads remind them of your gym and can nudge them to take the next step.

Optimize Lead Nurturing with Automation

Generating leads is just the beginning. You need to nurture those leads to keep them engaged until they're ready to commit. Automation tools make this process easier, ensuring you stay connected without spending hours on follow-up.

Consistent follow-ups through email and text automation are key.

Here's how to set it up:

- **Send Immediate Follow-Ups**: When someone signs up for a free trial or downloads your lead magnet, send an automated welcome email. This should introduce your gym and outline the next steps, like booking a consultation or starting a free trial.

- **Drip Campaigns**: Set up a series of automated emails to nurture leads over time. These can include fitness tips, client success stories, and special offers to encourage action.

- **Text Follow-Ups**: Text messages feel more personal than emails. Use them to send reminders, encourage free trial attendees to return, highlight upcoming events or make offers.

Winning at lead generation is about more than just attracting a lot of leads.

It's about attracting the right leads who will eventually become clients. By combining a variety of lead generation methods, you'll consistently bring in high-quality leads, month after month.

Key Takeaways:

1. ***Create Lead Magnets That Attract Quality Prospects****: Offer resources like free guides or trial programs in exchange for contact details. Make sure they align with your services to attract the right leads.*

2. ***Leverage Referrals****: Encourage your current clients to bring friends by offering incentives or running referral contests. This taps into your existing community for high-quality leads.*

Use Social Proof and Targeted Ads*: Share success stories and testimonials to build trust, and invest in targeted ads to bring in local leads.*

Chapter 7

Build Your Gym's Authority in the Community

What's it take to build your gym's trust in your market and to truly establish your gym as a fitness leader in the community? It's not just about having flashy equipment, being located in prime real estate or being the biggest gym around. It's about becoming a trusted resource and a pillar in your local community.

If you're not there yet—if people in your town don't see you as the go-to place for the outcomes you help people achieve, it's time to change that.

And it starts with you. So, let's talk about how you can build your gym's authority, step by step.

Own the Responsibility

The first step is simple: **take ownership**. I get it. It's easy to think, *"That gym down the street has the backing of a franchise,"* or *"They've got deeper* *pockets than I do."* But that mindset? It won't help you. Look, the best gyms in any market didn't just stumble into being the best. They took action. They owned their space, consistently showed up, and didn't wait for anyone else to validate them. If you want to build authority, you can't wait for someone else to give you permission. It's your job to create that reputation.

Commit to Continuous Improvement

Here's the thing: Great businesses didn't start off that way. They just got a little better each day.Now, someone might walk into your gym and think, *"This looks like any other training facility,"* and maybe on the surface, it does. But the difference is in the details.

The best gyms don't just stick with what works. They keep improving—1% at a time.You don't need to overhaul everything at once. But you do need to commit to getting better—whether it's refining your training systems, improving how your staff communicates, or tightening up your follow-up process. Those changes and tweaks add up. And over time, they compound.

Imagine this: You've got a referral program in place, and it's working. But instead of letting it run on autopilot, you focus on making it incrementally better each month.

Maybe you adjust the incentives. Maybe you find a more effective way to ask for referrals. Over time, that program goes from yielding 1-2 guests a month to helping you attract 6-8 new, qualified prospects.Over the course of a year, that one approach to getting better could yield an additional 30-40 clients.

That's the power of continuous improvement.

Get Involved and Stay Visible

You can't build authority from behind a desk. If you want people to know your gym, you need to be out there in your market. It's not enough to stay within the four walls of your gym.

You've got to get involved in the community—attend local events, partner with schools or sports teams, and collaborate with other local businesses. The more visible you are, the more people will associate your gym with leadership and positive impact.

Leverage Social Proof

Your reputation hinges on what people say about you - more now than ever before. The voices of your visitors are amplified by social media and reviews, making good reviews amazing and bad reviews disastrous. But here's the deal: Don't just hope for good reviews or testimonials. Ask for them. When a client has an amazing transformation, don't keep it in house. Share it. Ask them to leave a review or write a testimonial. Make it easy for them. Prospects are far more likely to trust you when they see others sharing real stories and real results.

Here's the simplest way to start: Make your google business profit a priority. Aspire to have the most reviews in your community and employ systems that turn clients wins into new reviews consistently.Social proof is powerful. Make it a priority.

Offer Expertise, Not Just Workouts

You're not just running a gym. You're offering solutions based on expert knowledge. People don't just need a workout. They need guidance on fitness, nutrition, recovery, and mindset. Position yourself as an expert—not just in exercise, but in overall wellness.Think about it: When people come to you for guidance, not just a workout, you're no longer just the gym down the street. You're the go-to expert they trust for their well-being.Whether it's through speaking in the community, your social media content or even writing a book—share your knowledge. The more value you offer, the more your authority grows.

Play the Long Game

Building authority doesn't happen overnight. You need to commit to the long game. That means showing up consistently and doing the work, even when results aren't immediate.

Here's the truth: A lot of gym owners say they're going to make changes. But how many actually follow through? The gyms that succeed are the ones that commit to action—again and again. Think about the compounding effect of small improvements. If your gym gets just 1% better each week—in how you train, market, or interact with clients—those changes add up. Before you know it, you're not just keeping pace with your competition—you're leaving them behind.

Bottom line: Building your gym's authority in the community isn't about having the best equipment or the fanciest space. It's about taking ownership, committing to improvement, and staying visible. It's about showing people you're here for them—not just to give them a workout, but to help them reach their goals.

Key Takeaways:

1. *Take Ownership of Your Reputation: Stop waiting for others to validate your gym—step into the spotlight and build your reputation. Attend community events, partner locally, and showcase your results to stand out.*

2. *Leverage Social Proof: Highlight client success stories and encourage Google reviews. The trust others have in your results will bring new clients through your door.*

Improve Daily: Commit to small, consistent improvements in your systems, communication, and training. The 1% gains compound into big results over time.

Chapter 8

Automate Your Marketing Efforts

The Key to Consistent Growth for Your Gym

Most gym owners have experienced being overwhelmed with their day-to-day responsibilities. Between running sessions, managing their team, and keeping clients happy, their marketing efforts always seemed to fall behind.

And I'll bet you've felt the same way.

Marketing can feel like another thing on your to-do list that never gets checked off. You know it's important, but when are you supposed to find the time to do it consistently? The answer isn't just to work harder or longer—it's to work smarter.

And that's where automation comes in. Automation isn't just about saving time. It's about creating consistency. It's about building a system that markets your gym even when you're not actively pushing every button. Let's talk about why automating your marketing is one of the smartest moves you can make.

Why Automation is Essential

When you hear *"automation,"* you might think of something impersonal or robotic. But here's the thing: automation doesn't have to take away the personal touch. But rather, automation enhances what you would have done manually by handling the repetitive tasks for you, freeing up your time to focus on what really matters—your clients.

Most gym owners are stuck in a cycle of manual marketing. They send emails one by one, post on social media when they remember, and follow up with leads only when they have a free moment. It's inconsistent. And inconsistency is the enemy of growth.

With automation, you can make sure your message goes out regularly without relying on bursts of energy or free time that never seems to come. You're always in control of your brand's narrative and building momentum, even when you're busy.

The Power of Consistent Messaging

Think about the most successful gyms in the industry. What's one thing they all have in common? Consistency.

They're consistently present in front of their audience. They don't just show up when they feel like it or when they have extra time. They've found a way to stay top of mind in their community, and that's no accident. Automation will help you do the same. Whether it's an email campaign, social media posts, or lead follow-ups, automation allows you to stay connected without needing to be glued to your phone or computer. You can use automation to follow up with new leads, build relationships, and consistently deliver offers. And this can happen in the background while you're coaching, running your gym, or spending time with family.

Turning Leads into Clients

You already know how important it is to follow up with leads. But let's be honest... if you're busy running a gym, you don't always have time to follow up as quickly as you'd like. The way you follow up matters. Studies show that businesses who follow up with leads frequently & consistently convert more leads into clients. But if you're with clients, following up in a family fashion can be a struggle. That's where automation saves the day.

With automation, you can set up a sequence that:

- Instantly sends a welcome message to every new lead, no matter the day or time.

- Follows up for a series of days with invitations, content, social proof & offers.

By automating this process, you ensure that no lead slips through the cracks, and every potential client gets the attention they need...without you having to lift a finger.

Personalized Marketing at Scale

One of the biggest myths about automation is that it's impersonal. But the truth is, automation allows you to deliver more personalized experiences at scale.

Let's say you're running different programs at your gym. You want to market to both young athletes and adults. With automation, you can create separate campaigns that speak directly to the unique challenges and goals of each group. With just a few tweaks, you can deliver highly personalized messages to different segments of your audience, all using the same automated system.

And it doesn't stop with email. You can do the same thing with targeted social media ads, automated texts, and even direct mail campaigns.

Keeping Clients Engaged

Automation isn't just for bringing in new clients. It's also a powerful tool for keeping the clients you already have. Once someone signs up for your gym, the work is just beginning. You need to keep them engaged, motivated, and excited about being part of your community.

Automated systems can help you:

- Send regular progress check-ins.

- Offer reminders when they miss a session.

- Share motivational success stories and client highlights.

You can even automate birthday messages, renewal reminders, and special offers for long-term clients. These little touches go a long way in building loyalty and showing your clients you care.

The Compound Effect

Like any good system, the power of automation comes from the **compound effect**. At first, automating a few tasks might not seem like a game-changer. But over time, these consistent, automated touches add up. Before you know it, you've built a marketing machine that's working for you around the clock.More leads. More clients. More growth. And all without the constant grind of manual marketing. But remember...automation doesn't replace the personal touch. It enhances it. By taking care of the repetitive tasks, automation frees you up to focus on what really matters: building relationships, delivering value, and making an impact. At the end of the day, automation isn't about doing less, it's about doing more with your time. It's about building systems that work for you, creating consistency in your outreach, and keeping your gym top-of-mind in your community.

Key Takeaways:

1. ***Streamline Follow-Ups:*** *Set up automated emails and texts to follow up with leads consistently. Automation ensures no lead falls through the cracks, saving you time while keeping your marketing proactive.*

2. ***Personalize at Scale:*** *Use automation to deliver tailored content to different audience segments. This keeps your messaging relevant without requiring extra manual effort.*

Stay Consistent: *Build an automated marketing system that runs even when you're focused on your clients. Consistency creates trust and ensures your gym is always top of mind.*

Chapter 9

Create Your Monthly Marketing Machine

Our Recommendation for Building a Rock-Solid Marketing Plan

If you picked up this book and flipped directly to this chapter, I wouldn't really blame you [but seriously, you should probably go read the other chapters too]. Marketing is tough.

Pulling in business from nowhere is tough. And most of the questions that first-time business owners ask have to do with marketing, and how they'll get new business through their gym door.

And just as you desired, in this chapter we are going to provide you with some marketing tools that are specific to a gym startup.

Drum roll, please...

Creating a Monthly Marketing Machine

For consistent gym growth, you need a reliable monthly marketing system - a machine that brings in new leads, retains current clients, and generates ongoing referrals.

Instead of scrambling month to month, building a monthly marketing machine ensures that your gym's marketing efforts run smoothly, automating key components while leaving room for personal interaction.

By incorporating referral marketing, local outreach, and digital strategies, you'll create a well-rounded system that delivers results.

Here's how to do it.

Step 1: Build a Monthly Marketing Calendar

The foundation of your marketing machine is a detailed monthly calendar. Your calendar should rotate between campaigns designed to attract new leads, engage existing members, and drive referrals.

Here's what that looks like:

- **Lead Generation Campaigns**: Run promotions to attract new clients, like free trials or low-barrier offers such as a discounted first month. This keeps your pipeline full and ensures new prospects are consistently engaging with your business.

- **Client Engagement Campaigns**: Keep current members excited with fitness challenges, specialty programs, or new offers. Engaged members are less likely to leave and more likely to refer.

- **Referral and Reactivation Campaigns**: Ask for referrals consistently, and run campaigns to bring back past clients. For example, once a quarter, you could focus on reactivating former members with a special offer.

By placing these activities into a calendar, you ensure that your marketing is proactive rather than reactive.

Step 2: Incorporate Referral Marketing

Referral marketing is one of the most powerful tools in your marketing machine.

Why? Because referrals come with built-in trust. Let's face it, referrals are usually the highest quality leads you can get.

Here's how to create an ongoing referral system:

- **Make Referrals Easy**: Make it simple for members to refer friends. Provide gift cards, text templates, or social media prompts they can easily share.

- **Offer Incentives**: Reward both the referrer and the new client. For instance, when a client refers a friend, send the referring client a gift and offer the referred guest a discount on their first month.

- **Referral Campaigns**: Run specific referral drives or referral contests. This keeps referrals top of mind and encourages a steady stream of new leads.

Referral marketing works best when it becomes a consistent part of your strategy.

Dedicate time each month to focus on referrals, and you'll build a strong, self-sustaining lead generation system.

Step 3: Automate and Schedule Marketing Activities

Automation is core to the monthly marketing machine.

Using tools like email marketing platforms, social media schedulers, and CRM systems, you can automate much of your marketing, saving time and ensuring consistent outreach.

Here are a couple examples of what you can do:

- **Email Campaigns**: Email is key for keeping leads and members engaged. Automate sequences for lead nurturing, member engagement, and referral reminders.

- **Social Media Scheduling**: Pre-schedule your social media posts to ensure a consistent presence. Highlight member success stories, promotions, and events. Combining organic posts with paid ads will expand your reach and drive engagement.

Automate what you can so you free up more time for personal interactions & local marketing while ensuring consistency.

Step 4: Leverage Local Marketing Opportunities

Digital marketing is important, but local marketing is equally crucial, especially for brick-and-mortar gyms.

Here are 3 ideas for ramping up your local marketing efforts:

- **Local Business Partnerships**: Partner with nearby businesses to run joint promotions or to deploy fish bowls for lead generation.

- **Community Events**: Sponsor or attend local events like health fairs, races, or charity events. Set up a booth or offer a fitness demo to engage directly with potential clients and build your brand in the community.

- **Local Advertising**: Print marketing like yard signs or postcards still works great when used properly.

Local marketing helps you build relationships with your community while raising awareness about your gym's services.

Step 5: Use Social Proof to Drive Conversions

People trust what others say about your gym more than what you say yourself. When people see others achieving results with your gym, they're more likely to believe they can achieve the same. Social proof, like testimonials and success stories, can be incredibly persuasive.

Here's how to use social proof:

- **Success Stories**: Regularly share member transformations. Whether through social media, email, or on your website, testimonials and before-and-after photos build trust and credibility.

- **Google Reviews**: Encourage your clients to leave positive reviews. These not only help boost your credibility but also improve your search engine rankings, making it easier for potential clients to find you.

Creating a monthly marketing machine isn't about throwing together random promotions. It's about building a structured, repeatable system that combines digital, referral, and local marketing to generate steady leads and retain your clients.

Utilizing Specialty Programs and Internal Offers to Attract New Members

Although paid advertising and local community outreach methods can be great ways to attract new members to your gym, if you're reading this book you most likely have an existing group of clients that want something new to keep them engaged and prevent boredom, but it can also be a great opportunity for them to refer and bring new members in.

So what is a Specialty Program?

A Specialty Program is a term for any one-off program that you put together, typically run by you or one of your team members that has a *"special"* interest in a particular topic.

It's not something that you want to be a part of your core offer 365 days a year, and it's largely dependent on that staff member running it.

Some great examples of specialty programs include:

- Kid's Programs

- Nutrition Programs

- 5k Prep Program

- Barbell Specialty Course

- Yoga/Mobility Course

The ideas are endless and I encourage you to go to your staff to see what their special interests are. Ask them what they would like to do that they are currently not able to do within the scope of personal training and group training. For this special interest program to work, your coach needs to be interested in it. Do not force them to be part of a special interest group that you create out of your own interests.

So how do you run a Specialty Program?

After you have a coach who is interested in a particular specialty program, I recommend you set up a meeting to discuss:

1. Length of program (I recommend 4-8 weeks)

2. Cost of program (I recommend around $29-49/week depending on the deliverables)

3. The deliverable of program (what is the client getting, what is the schedule, logistics, etc)

4. Financial structure for the coach (more on this in a minute)

5. Marketing of the program

From there, I recommend that you make it clear which tasks you'll be handling and which tasks you expect your coach to be handling. As the owner, it makes sense for you to handle the marketing and filling of the program. That means you can give your coach the responsibility of building out the deliverables and planning the actual program.

When it comes to payment, I would suggest that you split the revenue share 50/50. I consider this model to be appropriately generous, considering the fact that this program is not compulsory for your coach.

Marketing The Specialty Program

The way that you market your speciality group will either make or break it, so pay close attention. I would recommend that you start marketing the program about three weeks before it starts. Why? Because if you give your clients more time to plan they'll need reminders, and if you give them less time, they won't have a free slot in their schedule. Three weeks is perfect. Here's what you'll want to do to market your program:

- Put up flyers and a signup sheet in your gym

- Fit it into end-of-session announcements

- Make an event in your private Facebook group

- Make posts on social media

- Write emails about it

What is the benefit of running a speciality program?

In addition to providing you with a boost in revenue, a specialty program is designed to meet the following objectives:

1. Current clients not only spend more because they are paying to participate in this specialty program on top of their membership, but they are also excited for something new and exciting.

2. Allow clients to bring their friends, family, and co-workers to a new and exciting program.

3. Your coach is more engaged because they get to work on something that excites them. That not only benefits this specialty program, but the energy.

4. Signing up for a training membership can feel confusing, overwhelming, and intimidating. Signing up for a 4-week mobility class. Not so much.

5. You have the opportunity to wow these new recruits and convert them to your regular membership.

The Pitfalls of Specialty Programs

We've made it sound very easy and beneficial to start a speciality program, and for the most part it is but it is not foolproof. Let me share with you some of the mistakes that we made when we were just starting out, and running specialty programs:

1. Recurring programs don't work as Specialty Programs: These work best as one-time purchases, open-and-closed enrollment. You can certainly run them back to back and/or multiple times a year, but we get way more buyers when it's a one-time purchase vs a recurring add-on.

2. Coaches need to have a special interest in the program. The personal excitement of the coach to run the group is the key ingredient. For example, if you have a coach that loves nutrition, give them the structure to run an 8-Week Nutrition Program. However, understand that if that coach leaves the program will also stop. That's why we want these to be add ons, not a core part of your membership offerings

In summary, Specialty Programs can be a great way to boost current client engagement, get them to spend more, bring in new clients, and keep team members engaged.

Key Takeaways:

1. ***Build a Marketing Calendar****: Plan monthly campaigns for lead generation, client engagement, and referrals. Structure ensures your marketing stays proactive instead of reactive.*

2. ***Incorporate Referral Marketing****: Make it easy and rewarding for members to refer friends with contests and incentives. Referrals are your highest-quality leads.*

Leverage Automation*: Automate emails, social posts, and reminders to save time while ensuring consistency. Use tools to streamline your efforts and stay focused on building relationships.*

PART III

Convert

Turn Prospects into Clients

Chapter 10

Design a Compelling Sales Process

Creating a sales process is not just about closing deals and acquiring transactions. Yes, these things are important, but if you are going to have a sales process that creates lasting relationships, offers real solutions and keeps your customers coming back, then it needs to be compelling.

It has to resonate with your potential clients and guide them toward a solution they feel excited about.

So let's talk about designing a sales process that not only helps you convert clients, but also sets the stage for long-term relationships.

Sales is About Solving Problems, Not Closing

First off, stop thinking of sales as something you're doing *to* people. It's something you're doing *for* people.

The goal isn't just to get someone to pay for a membership or program. It's to engage in a win-win partnership that solves their problems and compensates you for your contribution to that.

Think about it this way: most people come to you with a specific goal in mind—they want to lose weight, get stronger, feel healthier, or maybe they just want to feel confident again.

Your role isn't to convince them to join a program; it's to introduce them to   the program that solves their problem. When you think of it this way, selling becomes a natural extension of coaching. You're not a salesperson; you're a guide who helps people achieve their goals.

That's the approach to both maximize new client growth while also building lasting relationships.

Step 1: Connect with People

Engagement is where it all starts.

You need to connect with people before they will even consider you as a potential solution. This step allows the prospect to get more comfortable in what is often an uncomfortable environment. Avoid the common mistake of jumping straight into the details. Prospects don't care about the details right away. They care about whether you can help them.You want to find common ground; something that puts them at ease and lets them know you're interested in them and their unique needs and goals.

Talk about family, sports, hobbies, anything that makes the conversation feel more natural. The trust you build here will set the tone for the entire conversation. Without that sort of trust, it makes the rest of the process more challenging.

One useful tip: try to match their energy level. If they're excited and energetic, meet them at that level. If they're calm and laid back, dial down your energy. This helps create an instant connection.

Step 2: Discover Their Motivations, Challenges and Needs.

Once you've engaged with the potential client, it's time for discovery. This is the part where you dig deeper into their motivations, challenges, and needs. It's all about asking the right questions to figure out what's important to them. A big part of discovery is positioning yourself as the expert. You're not just another trainer, you're the most qualified expert that can help them solve their problems & reach their goals.

But remember, being an expert doesn't mean bombarding them with jargon or talking over their heads. It means guiding the conversation in a way that makes them feel heard, understood, and supported.

Ask open-ended questions like:

- *"Why is this goal important to you?"*

- *"What's kept you from achieving this in the past?"*

- *"What would be a dream come true result for you?"*

By the end of the discovery phase, you should have a clear understanding of their needs and how you can help them.

Step 3: Build Value

Now that you know what they're experiencing and what they want, it's time to show them how you can help. This is where you connect the dots between their problems and your solutions. You're not just selling a training program—you're selling the transformation they're looking for.Explain how your training solutions are designed to address their needs & get them where they want to go. Use examples and success stories to demonstrate the value of your program. If you can show them how you've helped others in similar situations, it becomes easier for them to see how you can help them too.Remember, people aren't buying time or sessions—they're buying what those sessions will do for them. Focus on the outcome, not just the process.

Step 4: Present the Solution

Now, it's time to get specific. Once you've built the value, present the exact solution that fits their needs. Don't overwhelm them with options—keep it focused & prescriptive.

Here's a rule of thumb: Give them two to three options at most.

Too many choices can lead to indecision. Remember, a confused mind says no. Present two or three solutions that you think are the best fit based on the discovery process. When you present the options, be confident.

You've already demonstrated that you understand their problem and have a solution that will work for them. Now it's time to step up and guide them to the next step. Instead of asking, *"Do you want to join?"* lead the conversation with *"Based on what you told me, one of these would be the best option for you. Which would you like to get started with?"*

Step 5: Optimize the Relationship

The client has enrolled, but your job isn't over yet. In fact, it's just beginning. Now it's about optimizing the relationship and setting the stage for long-term success. Start by providing a seamless onboarding experience. Make sure they feel welcomed and supported from day one. Employ the new client onboarding process we discuss later.But most importantly, remember that this is the beginning of a transformational relationship instead of the end of a transaction.

Mastering the Follow-Up Formula

Imagine if every lead that came through your door provided you with a 10x better ROI than it is yielding today. That is the power of a strong follow-up formula. If we can have a stronger follow up for system for every lead you'll convert more leads to sales consultations, and we all know the famous gym owner saying:

"Once I get them in the door, they stay."

Converting prospects once they walk through our doors is usually not a challenge because the training gym product is so good and different from a traditional health club offering. That means, we need to put our focus on the follow-up. So where does it start?

It begins with having a strong lead tracking system. Now this doesn't need to be complicated. A simple spreadsheet of the name, contact info, method of reach out, and last contact is all you need. The key with this is it needs to be viewed and updated DAILY. If you take one thing away from this section, it's the understanding that *lead tracking and follow is a daily activity*. Determine who will be in charge of following up with leads on a daily basis. That might be you, if you're the type of owner who likes to personally connect with potential clients, or you might assign this to a respected and trusted employee.

As a lead comes in (regardless of method) it needs to be entered onto the lead tracker. If you'd like to take a cue from this book and automate this process, I would suggest using a service like Zapier Regardless of how you decide to follow up, you must do this rather quickly, as a recent survey published by HubSpot stated that most prospects expect a response within 10 minutes or they will move onto another similar service. So I would suggest that you set it up so that you receive a t notification (via text and/or e-mail) that a lead has come in.

If you can follow up with a lead as soon as it comes in, the chances of them actually converting to a sales consultation go through the roof.

So, how should I follow up with leads?

There are three methods of contacting a lead..

    1. Phone Call

    2. Text Message

    3. E-Mail

I recommend you use all three methods until they respond. After a lead comes in and is placed on the lead tracker, please pick up the phone and call them. ***Yes, call them.*** I know they are not going to answer. However, it is always best practice to call and leave a voicemail that sounds something like this:

"Hey, this is Doug over at Doug's gym. I received your inquiry for our program. I'd love to learn more about you and help you get started. I'm going to send you some information via text and email, go ahead and respond to one of those if it's easier. I can also be reached via phone at XXX-XXXX. Talk soon!"

The key in the voicemail is it puts a voice behind the brand. It shows the lead that you are real, that you are responsive, and when done right, they can hear your smile and how much you care, through the tone of the voicemail.

Not to be downplayed, it is also important to direct them to look for the text or email that could get lost.

Once you hang up the phone, I want you to text and email them as you said.

Now, if they respond, I want you to *"**marry the method.**"*

Meaning, if they respond via text keep the conversation going on text messaging If they respond via email, keep the conversation going on email.

Of course, not everyone is going to respond right away to your first set of reach outs, and that is where the real work of follow up begins.

I recommend a very simple EOD (every other day) follow up formula.

Using your lead tracker you simply check daily and ask yourself *"did I follow up with this person yesterday?"* If the answer is yes, then you can take today off. If the answer is no, then they need a follow up. If they haven't responded to any of your messages, I recommend you continue the layered approach of text, e-mail, and phone call for every follow up until they respond to one.

Don't assume they prefer one method of communication over another. Every person has a preference for communication methods (text, email, phone call), and you don't want to assume what it is until they respond to you.

Q: How long do you keep following up if they don't respond?

Until they respond, say no, or die. In all seriousness, this is the difference maker and will take a mediocre sales month to a great sales month.

Hub Spot says that for 80% of buyers, you will need to follow up about five times before they answer.

Now just think about it. If you currently have a sales process that involves follow up [I can't imagine that any business runs without one], how many times have you followed up only once or at the most thrice and then left it at that?

If you've done that in the past, you've likely lost about 80% of your sales!

Ok listen. It's ok. Today is a good day for a sales process overhaul. Stay aggressive with the EOD follow up method until they respond. Once they respond, move them to a sales conversation and direct them to whatever you step one is (assessment, success session, free trial, etc). That is the key to a strong follow up formula. Implement this and watch each and every lead become more valuable and your gym grow.

Final Thoughts

Creating a compelling sales process is about more than just closing sales.

It's about understanding your clients, building trust, and offering real, personal solutions.

When you approach selling this way, you'll not only see more success, but you'll also build stronger, longer-lasting relationships with your clients.

Remember, the best sales process doesn't feel like selling at all. It feels like helping.

And at the end of the day, that's exactly what you're doing: helping people reach their goals and improve their lives.

Key Takeaways:

1. *Focus on Solving, Not Selling*: *Approach sales as problem-solving rather than convincing. When clients feel heard and their problems addressed, enrollment becomes a natural next step.*

2. *Keep it Simple*: *Offer 2–3 solutions tailored to the client's needs. Too many options create confusion, and a confused mind says no.*

Optimize Relationships from Day One: *A great onboarding experience sets the stage for long-term retention. Make clients feel valued from their first interaction.*

Chapter 11

Master Memberships

Pricing Pricing Strategies for Profitability

Establishing the right pricing structure for your gym is one of the biggest challenges you'll face as a business owner. It's easy to think that lower prices will bring in more clients, but if you're not careful, you could end up discounting your way to bankruptcy. The key is to develop a pricing strategy that attracts clients while ensuring long-term profitability for your gym. The goal? Strike the balance between affordability and sustainability.

Here's how you can do it.

Understand Your Costs

Before you can set any prices, you need to know your costs inside and out. What does it take to run your gym every month? This includes rent, utilities, staff costs, equipment... everything. You need a clear picture of what's going out before you can figure out what should be coming in. A good rule of thumb is to aim for monthly revenue that's at least 2.5 times your operating expenses. This cushion allows you to cover costs, reinvest in the business, and leave room for profit.

For example, if your operating costs are $10,000 per month, your target revenue should be $25,000. Knowing your numbers gives you a solid foundation.

Without this understanding, you're just guessing - and that's risky.

Choose the Right Pricing Model

The pricing model you choose has to fit your gym's offerings and your target market.

There are a few proven models that work well in the fitness industry. These include:

- **1:1 High-End Private Training**: Personalized, premium service comes at a higher price, but it's a great model if your gym is focused on delivering tailored experiences.

- **Semi-Private Training (3:1 ratio)**: More scalable than 1:1 training but still personalized. It allows you to keep pricing competitive while managing more clients.

- **Small Group PT (4-6:1 ratio)**: This model lets you serve more clients per session while still maintaining a hands-on approach.

- **Large Group Classes (15-20+ members)**: These are lower-cost options for clients, but they require more space and staffing.

Your goal is to pick the model (or combination of models) that works best for your business and your market. Choose what aligns with your brand and what you can deliver with consistency. Don't try to be everything to everyone. Be the best at what you choose.

Offer Tiered Pricing Options

Tiered pricing is a strategy that allows you to serve different segments of your market, catering to clients with varying budgets while guiding them toward your most profitable offerings.

Here's an effective tiered structure:

- **Irresistible or Front End Offer**: This could be a trial membership or a basic package that lowers the barrier to entry. It's not about profit; it's about letting clients experience the value you offer.

- **Core Offering**: This is your bread and butter—your most common membership or package that should be priced based on your ideal average revenue per member (ARM). Most clients will choose this option, so it needs to provide both value and profitability.

- **Premium Offering**: This is for clients willing to pay more for additional services or exclusivity. Think personalized nutrition coaching, private training sessions, or VIP access to your facility.

By offering a tiered pricing structure, you cater to different client needs and maximize revenue by guiding clients toward the option that makes the most sense for them.

Focus on Value, Not Just Price

It's easy to get caught in a pricing war with competitors, but dropping your prices too low can lead to a race to the bottom. Instead of trying to be the cheapest, focus on communicating the value you provide. Clients will pay more when they understand the benefits they're getting. Don't just sell a membership - sell outcomes. Instead of listing how many classes you offer, focus on the results your clients will see. We recommend having a pricing menu that clearly outlines not only the cost but also the value in terms of results. A well-designed pricing menu shows clients the full picture of what they're investing in. Developing a profitable pricing strategy is all about balance. It's about understanding your costs, choosing the right pricing model, and offering tiered options that fit both your clients' budgets and your gym's financial needs. When done right, your pricing strategy can help you build a thriving, sustainable gym that continues to grow while delivering incredible value to your clients. Focus on outcomes, not just numbers, and make sure your pricing reflects the results your clients can expect. That's how you'll not only attract new clients, but keep them for years.

Offering Tiered Memberships and Upsell Opportunities

If you're running a gym, offering tiered memberships can be a game-changer. Not only does it give your clients options that meet their needs, but it also provides a clear path to upsell opportunities... helping you boost revenue in a strategic, sustainable way. When done right, tiered memberships allow clients to select the level of service that best suits them, while giving you a framework to offer additional value at higher price points.

It's all about scalability and encouraging clients to move up the value ladder over time.

Here's how to make tiered memberships and upselling work for your gym.

Understand the Value of Tiered Memberships

Tiered memberships aren't just about having a low, medium, and high-priced option. It's about clearly defining the value each tier provides. The key is understanding what different types of clients need. The idea is to offer packages linked to specific outcomes that your clients desire. Your pricing shouldn't just be based on the number of classes or access they get, it should be based on the results they're aiming to achieve.

Here's a simple breakdown:

- **Basic Membership**: This is **Tier 1:** Think of this as your lowest point of entry. It's going to include the lowest frequency you're willing to work with someone. Perfect for self-motivated clients who just need the sessions and the inherent benefits that come with them. This is usually 4-5 sessions per month of your training program. Only about 10-20% of your membership will be on this option.

- **Mid-Tier Membership**: **Tier 2**: This is going to be your most common membership, and it's what you will sell 70-80% of the time. This is what your ideal client wants and gives them the best chance of not only results but succeeding in the feeling that they are fully utilizing the membership (they don't feel guilty they are not using all of it).

Most commonly, this is 8-10 sessions per month of your training program.

Includes everything from the basic tier plus some additional services, frequency or accountability.

- **Premium Membership**: This is for the top-tier clients who want everything - and this also serves as a price anchor to increase the perceived value of the Basic & MId-Tier Offers. This is often unlimited for your training program, and you may even throw in some bonus things like an InBody scan or a nutrition consultation (more on that later). Only about 10% of your membership is going to be on this option.

Give Your Tiers A Name

I recommend you come up with names for the three tiers. If you've been in this industry for a while, you know that *"session counters"* can be a pain in the butt. It's a good idea to name these memberships because it helps the client feel like they're buying a membership to your facility and they are subscribing to the idea of being on a certain membership, not "I get X number of sessions per month."

In addition to naming your membership, I recommend the following policies behind the membership:

1. Price it weekly (more on pricing next) (ex: $79/week).

2. Bill every 4 weeks (you get a 13th payment each year).

3. Memberships should automatically renew, and they have to come to you to cancel.

4. Have a long-term commitment (6 or 12 months) and have a month-to-month option that is 20% higher.

By offering different levels of service, you allow clients to start where they feel comfortable and move up as they progress in their fitness journey and in their relationship with you.

What Should Be Included in Your Memberships?

Obviously, you'll offer your clients a certain number of training sessions as we outlined below, but what else? My recommendation is to add very little. Not because I don't want you to over deliver and give a great experience, but because it will overwhelm the clients and kill your profitability. We have to realize that there are some clients (the majority) that just want to show up a few days a week, work hard, and go on with the rest of their life. They don't want all the extras like check-ins, nutrition stuff, in-body scans, and the like. Now, I'm not saying you shouldn't have that stuff built out, but I would recommend having those as optional add-ons (more on that in another chapter). This way, for clients that don't value it, they don't feel like they're paying for something they're not using, and for clients that do not value it, we know if they pay extra for it, they are more likely to use it and take it seriously. Plus, it keeps your profit margins higher. The last thing you want is a lot of *"indirect labor"* costs. That means labor (payroll $$$) that is not on the floor training clients.

Upselling Without Being Pushy

Upselling works best when it feels like a natural progression, not a sales pitch. Clients need to see the next level of service as a clear and valuable upgrade from where they currently are.

Here's how to do that effectively:

- **Highlight Progress**: As clients start seeing results, they'll naturally want more. That's when you introduce the idea of upgrading. For instance, if someone in a basic membership is hitting their goals, you might say, *"You're doing great. Integrating nutrition coaching could help you get even better results faster."*

- **Use Testimonials**: Showcase success stories from clients who moved to a higher-tier membership and saw faster results. Real-life examples go a long way in helping people see the value of upgrading.

- **Offer Trials or Temporary Upgrades**: Give clients a taste of the next tier with a short-term upgrade. Let them experience the added benefits, making it easier for them to commit to a higher-level membership permanently.

Upselling doesn't have to be pushy. It's about showing clients the potential for greater success with additional services.

How to Price Your Memberships

I like to see training gyms make $200 per training session, ideally closer to $300.

- 1:1 High End Private Training: $100+/Hour (2+ Sessions Going On At Same Time)

- Semi-Private Training (3-4:1): $65+/session

- Small Group PT (4-6): $35+/session

- Classes (15+): $15+/session

Build an Upsell Infrastructure

Once you have your membership tiers, you need the right infrastructure to support upselling. Automation can play a big role in this. Automated systems can send tailored emails or notifications to remind clients about the benefits of upgrading.

This removes the pressure from your staff and ensures consistent messaging.

In addition to automation, train your team to recognize when a client is ready for an upsell. If you deliver consistent offers to your clients through automated content delivery and your team members are upselling clients who walk in your doors, then you'll see powerful results.

It allows you to meet clients where they are, providing them with the flexibility to choose what suits them best, while giving them a clear path to more personalized solutions as they progress. When done right, this approach increases client satisfaction and drives long-term profitability for your gym.

Key Takeaways:

1. *Know Your Numbers: Your revenue should be at least 2.5 times your operating expenses. Without clarity on costs, pricing becomes guesswork.*

2. *Offer Tiered Options: Create Basic, Mid-Tier, and Premium memberships to cater to different client needs while encouraging upgrades.*

Sell Outcomes, Not Features: *Clients don't buy sessions—they buy results. Frame pricing in terms of the transformation your gym delivers.*

Chapter 12

Great Events & Promotions

Running Successful Gym Events to Boost Memberships

We often think of marketing as things like sending emails, running paid advertising, or doing joint venture partnerships to generate leads. But what if I told you there is a strategy you can use to generate new clients each and every month, and the leads walk right in your door?

Let's talk through events to boost your membership.

Some of our best clients run monthly events that not only add a lot of value for current clients but also bring in the perfect prospect.

An example of a gym event that can be a great way to boost membership is seminars or workshops. These are one-time events where you're able to share your expertise (or bring in someone to) and convert walk-ins into clients.

The Framework

Pick your topic.

The topic needs to be something that BOTH you and your target market are excited about. Examples include nutrition topics, rehab/injury topics, mindset topics... really the idea is endless. It just needs to be a topic that gets people curious to learn more, and you can speak confidently about it. Once you have your topic, it's time to **pick your date and time.**

I recommend you pick a date that gives you two to three weeks of marketing runway. We typically find that a weekday evening works or a Saturday late morning. Now your market.

You could even survey your current clients. Once you pick your date, it's time to **pick your location.** Now, sometimes we have clients that feel they need to rent out a hall or use a bigger space for these, or even do them online. I want to stress that the magic is getting them in your space. They are able to get in the door, there's the mingling that happens before and after, and you are seen as even more of an authority because it's in your space.

Next up is your marketing.

Don't expect just to throw together a flier and have people busting down the door. We need to pull out all the stops. This includes...

- Flyers in your gym

- Announcements in your sessions

- FB Event

- Social Media Posts

- Social Media Ads

- Chamber of Commerce

- E-Mail List

- Flyers Around Town

- & More!

I recommended you ramp things up starting three weeks before the event, and keep up the push all the way until the day of.

Have a way for them to sign up ahead of time

This can be done electronically on a form and/or in person pen and clipboard style.

You want to send reminder texts and emails leading up to the event. Plus, if they don't show, you're still able to follow up.

Should you charge for Events?

A common question is, *"should you charge for these?"* My belief is no. I don't want any barrier to getting people to walk in my door. Make it as easy as possible. Plus, when done right, you're going to make out in the end.

How to Attract New Members?

You want as many current clients to show up as possible. Not only do they get added value in learning about the topic, but you're going to invite them to bring a friend. It's their chance to show off their gym. This acts as an amazing win, as not only do they bring people in, they sell them when they are there, telling them how awesome their gym is. You could even incentivize them to bring a friend by entering a raffle, giving them a discount off their next month, or giving them a free upgrade on their membership for the next month.

The Day of the Event

Deliver value on the front end, educate and motivate them. Then, at the end, have an offer for everyone there to try out your services. It could be an offer like a 14 Day Test Drive or a 28 Day Jumpstart. I recommend you limit it and give them a massive discount (70-80%).

We all know once they start training with you, they're going to have a great experience and will want to stick around. Some of our clients have really seen success while running these events; so much so that some even run these events once a month.

Now go get it scheduled and take action.

Utilizing Seasonal Promotions and Flash Sales to Drive Growth in Your Gym

Seasonal promotions and flash sales can be a game-changer for your gym, bringing in new clients, boosting revenue, and establishing your gym as the go-to place in your community. But it's not just about offering a discount and hoping for the best. It's about being strategic and intentional, and focusing on long-term success, not just a quick influx of cash. Let's dive into how you can use these tools to drive real growth for your gym.

Start with Strategy, Not Discounts

Here's the thing: a lot of gym owners think a flash sale means slashing prices to get a bunch of new clients in the door. But that's not the best approach. *It's not about cutting prices—it's about increasing value.* Before you offer any kind of discount or promotion, take a step back and ask yourself:

- What's my goal with this promotion?

- Who am I targeting?

- How can I make this offer a no-brainer while still maintaining the value of my services?

Let's say you're considering offering a steep discount.

Instead of simply cutting prices, why not consider bundling your services into a seasonal package? For example, you could run a Transformation Program that includes small group training, nutrition coaching, and accountability. By bundling services and enhancing the overall experience, you're not just offering a discount, you're offering real value that positions your gym as a premium option.

Leverage Seasonal Patterns to Your Advantage

The fitness industry runs on seasonal patterns. Think about it: New Year's resolutions, the lead-up to summer, back-to-school season... these are times when people are already looking for fitness solutions.

Instead of passively waiting for clients to walk through your door, capitalize on these moments.

Here's how:

- **New Year's Transformation Challenge:** People are motivated to make changes in January. Use this time to launch a 4 to 8-week challenge that helps them build momentum and moves them into being long-term clients.

- **Summer Ready Program:** As summer approaches, everyone wants to get in shape for vacations. Offer a *"Summer Ready"* Program that helps clients hit their goals while positioning your gym as the solution for quick, effective results.

- **Back-to-School Special:** When kids head back to school, parents often get a little more time to focus on themselves. Run a back-to-school promotion aimed at busy parents who need a flexible training program that fits into their schedule.

By aligning your promotions with natural seasonal motivations, you're tapping into desires that are already there. You're not creating urgency from scratch... you're amplifying it.

Create Urgency with Flash Sales

Let's talk about flash sales. These are powerful because they create a sense of urgency.

People act when they know the clock is ticking. But here's the key: a flash sale isn't just about offering a discount. It's about getting people to take action right now. Here's how to make it work:

- **Keep it short**: Flash sales should last 24 to 72 hours, max. The tighter the window, the greater the urgency.

- **Communicate clearly**: Make sure your audience knows exactly what they're getting, why it's valuable, and when the offer ends. Whether it's through email, text, or social media, your message should be crystal clear.

- **Tie it to an event**: Flash sales tied to specific events—like your gym's anniversary or a member milestone—create a natural reason for celebration and urgency.

For example, you could run a **Two-Day Anniversary Flash Sale**, offering new clients their first month at a special rate if they sign up on the anniversary of your gym's opening.

Or, you could offer a flash sale on nutrition coaching to celebrate reaching 10000 sessions delivered. The possibilities are endless—just make sure the offer is compelling, and the urgency is real.

Combine Promotions with a Strong Call to Action

No matter how great your promotion is, it won't work if people don't know what to do next. Your call to action needs to be clear, direct, and easy to follow. Whether you're promoting a summer challenge, a New Year's special, or a 24 hour flash sale, make sure your audience knows:

- What they're getting: Be specific about the features and benefits.

- When it expires: Emphasize the limited time of the offer.

- How to claim it: Tell them exactly how to sign up, whether it's through a landing page, a phone call, or an email.

Here's an example of a clear call to action:

"Our Summer Ready Program is open for enrollment now!

You'll get six weeks of small group training, nutrition coaching and personal accountability for just $299.

But this offer is only available until Sunday...reply with SUMMER to reserve your spot!"

Short, direct, and to the point.

Focus on Long-Term Retention, Not Just Short-Term Gains

Here's where most gyms miss the mark: they treat seasonal promotions and flash sales as a way to make a quick buck. But the real goal? Use these promotions to build long-term relationships. If you bring in new clients at a discount, your goal should be to win them over with your service, so they stick around long after the promotion ends.

Here's how:

- **Over-deliver on value**: Make sure your new clients feel like they're getting more than they expected. If you exceed their expectations in the first month, they'll be more likely to stick around.

- **Engage them quickly**: Have a structured new client onboarding system.

- **Provide a clear path forward**: Before their initial program ends,

have a conversation about their next steps. Make an offer, include
an incentive and transition them to becoming a long-term client.

By focusing on retention, you're turning a short-term promotion into a
long-term client relationship. Seasonal promotions and flash sales are tools
that can drive real growth for your gym if used strategically. Focus on
adding value, creating urgency, and building long-term relationships, and
you'll see your gym's authority grow…along with your client base.

Maximizing Conversions from Free Trials

While there are plenty of opinions on the topic, the truth is that offering
free trials is a great way to get prospects through the doors of your gym.
If you have a great experience to offer, it can be one of the strongest sales
tools you have at your disposal. Here's how you can maximize conversions
from free trials and build a stronger, more engaged member base.

Make the Free Trial An Experience

A free trial shouldn't feel like just another drop-in class that many facilities
offer. You need to make it clear to these prospects that they're stepping into
something unique, a real experience as a client in your gym. The mistake a
lot of gym owners make is treating a free trial like it's a generic session and
is something less than a paid session. If you do that, you've missed a huge
opportunity.

Instead, treat them like they're a five star prospect. Send a pre-trial email
that explains what they can expect, offers a tour, and introduces them to
key team members. Make sure they know they're getting more than just

access to a session. From the moment they walk through the door, they should feel special. Greet them by name.

It's all about building that initial connection, so they feel like they're already part of the community.

Personal Interaction Matters

People don't start programs just for the equipment, they join because they want to achieve the results that you said were possible because of your program. And a lot of the time, they also want to be part of the community that your gym has.

That's why personal interaction is key during a free trial. But understand that the trial should be a structured conversion process, so be sure to schedule a consultation on day one. Meet with the guest and ask what they're looking to achieve, what's worked for them in the past, and what hasn't. This gives you insight into how to best serve them and also shows that you care about their individual goals.

Then, follow up after each session. This builds rapport and makes them feel valued. You're not just offering a workout, you're offering a support system.

Show the Path Forward

Once they're in the free trial, don't leave them wondering what to do next. The biggest mistake you can make is letting them walk out the door without a clear sense of the next steps. They need a coach.

Here's what you can do:

- **Create a Plan**: Sit down with them after their trial and review their experience. Talk about their goals and how your gym can help them get there. Make it personal and specific to their needs.

- **Offer Options**: Give them a few membership options that suit where they're at. We recommend 2-3. Some people are ready to commit to a full membership right away, while others may need a short-term program to ease into it. Having a tiered offering can make the decision easier.

By doing this, you're not just selling them a membership, you're offering them a solution to the outcome they want.

Create Urgency

People are more likely to act when they feel like they're getting something that won't be available for long.

That's where creating urgency comes in. Offer limited-time promotions that encourage trial members to convert quickly. This could be:

- A waived enrollment fee if they sign up within 48 hours.

- A free nutrition coach program if they commit to a membership right away.

- Access to benefits that only clients get.

The key here is not to push too hard but to make it feel like they're getting an exclusive offer by acting now. It's a delicate balance, but done right, it works.

Automate Your Follow-Ups

Not everyone is going to convert on day one, and that's okay. Set up a follow-up system that works in tandem with the training sessions that builds value, persuades and reinforces the offer.

Remind them of the limited-time bonuses of discounts too.

Offer Two Deadlines

To improve your conversions, offer a *'fast action'* option for those who join within the first 24-48 hours and a second conversion offer that expires at the end of their trial.

Convert Them Now - Or Later

Yes, the goal is to convert free trials into paying clients now, but if they don't convert now it doesn't mean they won't ever become clients. People have any number of different variables that factor into their decision making, so if the timing isn't right now, that's ok. Follow up with them and when they're ready, they'll choose you. Converting free trials into long-term clients isn't about high pressure sales or just about getting them to sign on the dotted line. It's about delivering an experience that makes them want to stay. And once they enjoy that, the decision to join becomes easy.

Key Takeaways:

1. ***Leverage Events for Leads***: *Host workshops or seminars to bring prospects into your gym. These events build authority and let*

attendees experience your culture.

2. ***Make Attendance Easy****: Remove barriers like fees to maximize attendance. Focus on delivering value to win over new members.*

Incentivize Referrals*: Encourage current members to bring friends with raffles or discounts. A personal endorsement is your best marketing tool.*

PART IV

Deliver

Grow Through Client Results & Experience

Chapter 13

Optimize Gym Operations

Creating Efficient Scheduling & Attendance Systems

There are two types of gyms out there: the ones that enforce scheduling and the ones that allow their clients to drop in. From a consumer perspective, the drop in style of gym membership can be easier to slot in whenever, but this is not a very helpful or stable model to build a thriving gym business from.

So what am I saying? You need to build your gym around scheduled programs and scheduled one-on-one sessions with trainers. It's important and I'll tell you why: There is no better feeling than to know when a client is coming through the door. Your team can be ready to pull out all the stops when they have an efficiently run calendar to look at.

For years, I surveyed my clients trying to ascertain what they found most valuable and what made them feel most held accountable.

Time and time again, the number one thing that came up was...

"I have an appointment, it's in my calendar, and I know someone is waiting for me."

So simple, yet so powerful.

You might be thinking, boy, this is not rocket science. And you're right, it's not. Scheduling sessions in the training gym world is common, but it's not super common in the fitness industry.

We can build out all the accountability systems in the world, the best programming, and the best client experience, but at the end of the day it's the appointment in their phone that is most valuable.

Let me show you how to use the simple power of scheduling to your advantage.

Clients schedule themselves.

Gone are the days (hello 2009) of it being a *"value add"* for you to schedule sessions for clients. Clients want extreme convenience and flexibility. Of course, they can't just show up whenever they want, but they want the convenience of coming at varying times, and they want to schedule on their own. So what you want to do is introduce a scheduling structure to how your gym is run, but also allow your client to make their own appointments. This can be easily done by researching and signing up for a scheduling or customer relationship management application.

Organizing the Sessions Offered

Ok, now let's discuss how you can organize the session slots that you offer to your clients via these CRM apps. By incorporating these

well thought out processes you are [hopefully] avoiding the dreaded 50% attendance rate.

You're going to want your sessions to have a cap on them, but that the client cannot see those details when booking.

Have a waitlist feature on your app where people can add themselves to the waitlist for that time.

Schedules change, things pop up, and for whatever reason they need to take themselves out.

Those on the waitlist will get a text and email if they get bumped in (again, a standard feature on the major apps nowadays).

Have a **clear window** where the session *"closes"* for sign ups. This means that there is a date where your clients can no longer sign up to be part of that session. And they also cannot remove themselves.

Figure out your **scheduling rhythm**. This is when you release your next block of schedule. I don't recommend having an *"open"* or *"ongoing"* schedule. In that type of model, every time you need to make a change you are seen as the bad guy/gal.

Not to mention, you rarely evaluate if a time is still desirable/needed or if you need to add new times.

By having a scheduling rhythm (I recommend quarterly) you are able to pause and evaluate every 90 days to ensure that what you have for a schedule is best. Additionally, it gives you a rhythm to communicate about your schedule. This can include updates and changes, but also reminders on the waitlist or windows.

Programming That Retains Members

This is a section where you might actually feel like saying, *"I got this."* Maybe programming is one of your wheelhouses.

But what if I could get you to think about programming through a different lens? Instead of thinking about it from the *"X's & O's"* or through the results lens... what if you thought about how it can be used to retain members.

Because let's face it, you can have the best program in the world, but if the client leaves, they are no longer doing that program

Variables To Consider: Length of the Program

This can be one of the most difficult aspects of programming to nail out, because oftentimes our coaches or fitness instructors will come to us saying that the clients will achieve better results if they are engaged in the program longer. And this is probably true, but there are other pitfalls that you have to consider: 1) Clients will get bored if they are doing the same program for too long. And then they won't show up. 2) Clients will become discouraged at the lack of results if they work hard for a number of weeks but don't see the results they hoped for.

I recommend you put clients on 3-4 week programs.

Variables To Consider: Attaching Themes

Each cycle or rotation of your scheduled programming could have a theme. Try to have fun with this, and base your chosen themes on what you know of your clientele.

One cycle could be *"Welcome To The Gun Show"* with a special focus on arms, and the next cycle could be *"Quadzilla"* with a focus on legs. This keeps it interesting and allows you to market your programming.

Variables To Consider: Hype it Up

Don't just let your programs happen! Hype them up!

Put it on display and get clients excited by posting it in your members-only group, building up excitement to the next program *"getting released,"* and more.

Variables To Consider: Show them they are progressing!

The final thing I would consider with programming is to use it to help retain clients and **show them that they're making progress.**

It's very important to remember that clients don't live and breathe this stuff like you do.

They often just show up, work hard, and go home.

Sometimes they can pick their head up and think...

"Am I getting results?" As trainers, we're often making changes, seeing small improvements, and taking notes to progress them... but they don't see that. That leaves them blind to the process, and when they're blind to

the process, they assume the worst. At the same time, we don't want to overwhelm them and they don't care about the details... they just want to see they are getting better.

The best way to do this is to give them a visual representation of their progress. One of our clients sends their clients a screenshot every 90 days of a line graph that shows the upward trajectory of a handful of exercises they have gotten stronger in.

Another gym owner has clients complete a self assessment (1-10 scale) on things like sleep, stress, and energy, and then has them complete that same self assessment again every 90 days.

You can do this through technology or not, what's important is you build out a **system to show them results.**

Implement these three things into your programming system and watch your client satisfaction and retention improve.

Maintaining Facility Standards and Safety

Did you know that one of the reasons clients leave a gym is because of the facility's lack of cleanliness?

Now, I know you might think your gym is clean and safe, but just in case, let's review how you maintain your facility.

Free up Space: Deal with Clutter

The first part of facility standards and safety is making sure your gym is clutter free. You all have the equipment in the corner that only one person uses. Get rid of it.

Take the time to declutter and get rid of any equipment that is not used on a weekly basis.

Organize Your Equipment

From there, I want you to try to organize your equipment so it presents well to clients. That includes putting all your free weights on shelves and wall mount as much as you can to free up valuable floor space. I know that's not "cleanliness" specifically, but it helps clients perceive the gym as clean.

Have a daily, weekly and monthly cleaning checklist.

If you want to stay on top of the maintenance and cleanliness of your facility, you and your team need to be organized and prioritize these tasks.

For your daily cleaning checklist, I want you to focus on these three areas:

1. Bathrooms

2. Lobby

3. Floors

Bathrooms need to be cleaned daily, and sometimes even multiple times a day. Your entryway and lobby has the most traffic, changing of shoes, etc. It needs to be cleaned daily.

Finally, your floors need to be moped and or vacuumed daily. This should be part of someone's daily job.

For a weekly **cleaning checklist**, I recommended dividing your gym into sections, or *"zones"* as we called it. Each day, your team focuses on cleaning a particular zone. For instance, Monday is zone one, Tuesday is Zone two, etc.

This is your opportunity to do a deeper clean of your gym, get rid of the cobwebs, dust the shelves, etc.

Side note: I'm not as worried about the *"wiping down"* of things like mats, dumbbell handles, etc. That stuff is hopefully happening every day naturally as clients tidy up after themselves.

Finally, to complete the facility, I recommend a **monthly maintenance list.**

This is a checklist to go through all equipment that requires routine maintenance. Stability balls are blown up, no loose handles, no ripped bands or pads, etc.

Important note: I recommend that you map all of these checklists out on a laminated piece of paper and then have them posted in client facing areas of your gym

Why? The team is going to remember to do it AND clients will see the cleaning checklist, which is a confidence booster. Remember, germs and dirtiness is a real fear of clients. Keep your facility clean through these checklists and SHOW them that you're keeping it clean.

Considering the Safety of your Gym

I want you to maintain three important things:

1. Good workers' compensation

2. Good liability insurance

3. A working AED

Coming from someone who had a gym that had to use an AED on a client, and it literally saved their life...

Get the AED.

Key Takeaways:

1. *Leverage Scheduling Systems: Implement a client-driven scheduling system for efficiency and accountability. Empower clients to book their own appointments to improve attendance and satisfaction.*

2. *Streamline Maintenance: Create daily, weekly, and monthly cleaning and maintenance checklists. Cleanliness and organization build trust and retention.*

Prioritize Safety and Compliance: Ensure your gym has workers' compensation, liability insurance, and a working AED. These essentials protect your clients and business.

Chapter 14

Building a Winning Team

Hiring and Onboarding the Right People

To build a winning team, we need to bring on the right people.

But where do you find them, and how do you do that?

Here's a snapshot of the tasks that you'll need to complete to find the right staff:

1. Write up a Job Posting that will attract the type of employees you want to attract. [Create an offer]

2. Market the offer on multiple platforms

3. Sell them to join your program

4. Onboard and train them

Let's break that down.

Creating & Marketing Your Job Posting

During this step, you are marketing your gym, its values and goals, and the employee atmosphere you want to give, plus the job. You need to create this based on the type of people you want to attract.

I recommend you put together a sales page for your job.

This sales page can live on a URL such as yourwebsite.com/jobs.

This sales page should talk about what it's like to work at your company, what the job entails, and most importantly, what type of person are you looking for.

Don't go into details such as pay or schedule, just speak to the type of person you want.

At the bottom of this page, I recommend a short form where they can apply. The form should include their name, contact info, and maybe a short question about why they are applying.

A common mistake is we narrow the *"top of the funnel"* too much, we make it too hard to apply.

Once the page is created, you need to market it on different platforms.

This distribution should include e-mails to your list (clients and non-clients), social media, job platforms such as Indeed, texts sent to your contact list, etc. But remember to drive all of this traffic to the one job posting link you created above.

Start with a Phone Interview

I recommended a quick phone interview to weed out the applicants that you don't want to pursue. This is where you can be picky. If they pass the phone interview, bring them in for an in-person to meet the team.

I always tell my clients to hire for cultural fit and train later if you have to. That means, if you get the sense that the person you're interviewing would fit in well with the rest of your staff and believes the same things you do about how to treat your clients, how to properly represent your brand and vision for the business, then that's essentially a green light as far as I'm concerned. But I'm going to talk about this more in the next chapter, so hang tight.

Once you have your candidate and you offer them the job... close the deal :)

Your Onboarding Program

Once they are on the team, I recommend mapping out a 6-8 week onboarding program.

Each week should have a combination of on the floor training and "classroom" time where they are with you learning the ins and outs of their job and the company. For on-floor training, I recommend a training model that I call co-coaching.

Instead of shadowing, which can often feel boring and not very confidence-boosting for the new team member, co-coaching is progressive. In the beginning, they start with a small section of one client's workout, and each day you give them more and more responsibility, increasing each week.

For the *"classroom"* time, I recommend 10% of their week be off the floor with you/the manager. This time needs to be scheduled and each week should have a *"theme."* One week you may be going over the programming system, and the next week may be going over how you modify it for a client's knee injury.

The key is that the classroom time is scheduled, not random. Take the time to map out at least 6-8 weeks of this.

Checking in on Employees, Especially New Hires: The 5-15 Meeting

I highly recommend that every gym owner has what I call a 5-15 meeting, which is a 1:1 meeting with each team member on a weekly basis.

It involves answering five questions at the end of each week (we used a Google Form for this) and attending a standing fifteen minute meeting at the beginning of the week.

The form should be short and punchy, remember this is a weekly task, so keep the process efficient. You're doing this every week, so it doesn't need to be a lot.

The frequency and rhythm is what is important.

The five questions can be checking in on wins from the week, any struggles they hit, and maybe even a personal question. This is the time to praise things they are doing well, and even fit in a mini training session on something that they may not be doing up to par.

The fifteen meeting should be standing and casual.

Don't change the time each week, pick a time that both you and your employee can commit to each week.

I promise, if you do, you'll have an amazing team member that creates an enormous amount of value for your business.

Key Takeaways:

1. ***Hire for Culture, Train for Skills***: *Look for candidates who share your gym's core values and vision. Build a structured onboarding program to ensure alignment and growth from day one.*

2. ***Create Paths for Growth***: *Regularly meet with employees to set personal and professional development goals. Investing in their growth fosters retention and high performance.*

3. ***Lead by Example***: *Demonstrate commitment to improvement and growth through your actions. Transparent leadership builds trust and inspires the team.*

Chapter 15

Create a Team Culture Focused on Growth and Retention

Creating a thriving team culture within your gym is the cornerstone of long-term growth and retention. A high-performing team doesn't just operate efficiently—they embody a culture that drives personal and professional development, which in turn improves the member experience and reduces turnover. In this chapter, we'll explore how to create a culture that fosters growth and retention, focusing on both the internal team dynamics and the member journey.

1. Start with Your Gym's Core Values

Your gym's core values should be more than just words on a wall. They need to be the foundation of every decision and interaction within the team. These values set the tone for expectations and behavior, creating a shared sense of purpose.

For example, at my gym one of our values is curiosity. We wanted every team member to be curious.

That included while we were meeting new clients, during team meetings when we were brainstorming ways to improve things, or in moments of frustration with another team member.

We would often use the saying *"when you're furious, get curious."*

The key with values is to constantly talk about them, reinforce when they are not happening, and call out when they are happening.

Every example always comes back to a value...

2. Hire for Cultural Fit, Train for Skills

As I already said in the previous chapter, you can always train someone on the specifics of a role, but you can't change their fundamental values or attitude. When building a team focused on growth, it's essential to hire individuals who align with your gym's culture.

The interview process should prioritize assessing whether a potential hire shares your values and is motivated to grow both personally and professionally. I would recommend that you place more importance on getting to know them and not their certifications. Learn to care more about personality fit than you do scale fit.

Once you have hired the right people, commit to training them thoroughly. Provide them with the tools they need to succeed in their roles but also in their development as professionals. Create opportunities for cross-training and continuing education to keep your team engaged and growing. For example, you could arrange for weekly team meetings where you role play scenarios, or read a book together and brainstorming ways you can implement some of the actions into your gym.

3. Be a Good Leader

Leadership plays a critical role in fostering a growth culture. So, it's important that you understand how to be a good leader of your management teams, and all of your employees as a whole. Here are a few general beliefs I have about what it means to be a good leader:

1. Seek Out Development Opportunities Often

2. Be authentic: Adopt your own style of leadership

3. Be clear about your vision and goals

4. Get to know your people.

Seek out Development Opportunities Often

If you want your team to focus on improvement, retention, and development, you must demonstrate that commitment yourself. Regularly invest in your own leadership development and openly share your journey with your team. When they see you striving for improvement, it encourages them to do the same. Encourage open communication, acknowledge mistakes as learning opportunities, and celebrate wins—both big and small.

Leading by example also involves being approachable and fostering an environment where feedback flows freely in both directions. Team members should feel empowered to contribute ideas for how to improve the gym's operations and member experience.

Be authentic: Adopt your own style of leadership

We all probably have our favorite coach or mentor that we admire, and there are probably people that you think of when you think of good leaders, but don't try to be like them.

Be clear about your vision and goals

The second thing is to be clear on where you want to go, in terms of vision for your company. What changes do you hope to see in five years, ten years and beyond? Here are a few more questions you should think about:

- What kind of business do you want to have?

- How big?

- How many clients?

- Who do you want to serve?

- What kind of impact do you want to have?

The clearer you can get on your vision and goals for the future, the easier it is to lead. Because at the end of the day, leadership is all about getting your team excited about the vision and encouraging them to be a part of building it.

Get to know your people.

Get to know your people on a personal level, connect with them, get to know what they do for fun outside of work, and learn what makes them tick. The more you can get to know them the more they'll trust you, and leadership is all about trust.

4) Delegate to the right people

Good management starts with making sure every person on your team has clear roles and responsibilities.

These are the qualities *that you want in your* management *team:*

- They should know exactly what they need to do on a daily and weekly basis.

- They should understand the difference between excelling and doing the minimum required work.

- Able to teach employees based on the established system and not from their own experience or perspective.

These are their responsibilities:

- They should be documenting interactions as much as possible (pre-session flow, onboarding steps, etc.).

- Give employees a daily and weekly checklist of tasks to ensure that everything is getting done.

5. Create Clear Growth Paths

One of the biggest factors in retaining high-quality employees is providing them with a clear path for growth. Team members want to know that they're not just clocking in and out every day but are actively working toward bigger goals. I recommend you host "roadmap" sessions with team members every six months. These meetings are casual, usually over coffee or lunch, and it's designed to get to know them, where they want to go personally and professionally, and map out actionable steps they can take to get there. By supporting their growth, you'll retain top talent and build a stronger team that's dedicated to the success of your gym. Your team is on the front lines of member interactions, so their attitude and engagement directly influence whether members feel welcome and supported. When your staff genuinely enjoys their work and feels connected to the gym's mission, members are more likely to stick around, increasing retention and member satisfaction.

Building a team culture that focuses on growth and retention is an ongoing process, but it starts with clear values, strong leadership, and a commitment to investing in your people. By creating a work environment where team members are encouraged to grow and thrive, you'll not only build a high-performing team but also improve member satisfaction and retention, driving the long-term success of your gym.

Key Takeaways:

1. *Anchor Culture in Core Values*: Reinforce your gym's values in every decision and interaction. A value-driven culture keeps the team united and focused on long-term goals.

2. *Foster Collaboration*: Encourage open communication and celebrate successes. Building relationships within the team strengthens your retention strategy.

Develop Leadership Skills: Provide resources and mentorship to grow leaders within your team. Strong leadership drives retention and elevates the member experience.

Chapter 16

Enhancing Member Experience

Crafting a Client Onboarding Process that Wows

Streamlining the Membership Process

The process that you have in place for new members to join your gym should be smooth, simple and include minimal steps for the client to take. This might sound very obvious to you, but I can't tell you how many gym owners we've coached that just needed to simplify their new member process. The membership process should be smooth and simple.

For example, one of the biggest mistakes gym owners make is they make it too hard for someone to get started. For instance, One of our clients, when they first started working with us, had a two page questionnaire for someone to fill out before they walked in the door, and then two separate meetings before they could start working out.

We quickly changed that!

I'm all for getting to know a new client, and I'm by no means recommending that you just throw them into your program, but it is important that you can certainly streamline and simplify the way you do it.

Setting the First Appointment

Let's start at the beginning of the process.

When a lead comes in, they should be followed up with to schedule a single appointment. The entire goal of your follow up (text, e-mail, and phone calls) should be to schedule the first appointment either by phone call or an in person meeting. I would suggest that if your pricing is less than $200 per month then a phone call is sufficient. If not, then it's better to have the new member come in for an in person appointment. that appointment.

How many appointments do you need per week to hit your growth goal?

That appointment (we called our a Success Session) can happen in two different formats:

- A phone call (if your pricing is less than $200/mo this is sufficient)

- An in-person meeting (you will always sell more in this format)

Once that appointment is scheduled, I recommend that you send them daily content that will show them social proof of your service and what they can expect once their membership is active.

However, be sure that the prospective client doesn't have to do anything before the appointment. Other than consuming the content, they don't need to do anything until that appointment.

At that appointment you'll get to know them, do any movement assessment you deem appropriate, and sell them to a membership.

Q: How Can I Prepare for this appointment?

The only thing you need at that appointment is a registration form or a tablet.

You'll use the registration form or tablet (pulling up your client management software profile section) to take notes that are necessary for the team to know about the client and notes that are relevant to their programming, injuries, etc.

This can also include your liability waiver (have this built by an attorney) and the membership agreement. Your membership agreement should have your specific membership policies, and I recommend you have them initial next to each policy (scheduling, billing, etc). It's very important to be direct and clear, as this will reduce the amount of issues that you experience with this client down the line. Once you feel that you've captured enough of their information, do any movement assessment you deem appropriate, and sell them to a membership. Once the sale happens, the form is complete and stored electronically in their profile (if you didn't already use 100% electronic).

At that point, the sale is complete, and onboarding begins.

Check out the chapter titled *"Enhancing A Member Experience"* where I outline all the details of the onboarding program.

Onboarding Clients

So you just signed up a client. They swiped their credit card, signed their waiver, and are all scheduled for their first training session. Now what?

Well, it's time to onboard them! But what does onboarding even mean?

Onboarding is NOT just an automated email campaign that drips them fitness and nutrition tips. That's not what they need. At this stage of the game, they most likely have a few emotions...Nervous, scared, and intimidated, and a bit of buyer's remorse always kicks in. A good onboarding program aims to eliminate all those emotions. As soon as the client leaves, I recommend you do three things:

1. Immediately send them a welcome email that has a video (less than a minute) of what to expect on their first day.

2. Mail them a handwritten thank you note.

3. Confirm they are scheduled, update any notes in your client management software, and ensure everything is set up on the back end for them correctly.

The welcome email is so powerful. It not only gives them confirmation of signing up, but eases their anxiety of what to expect on day one. The handwritten thank you note is a game-changer.

When was the last time you got a handwritten thank you note in the mail? Years, if ever, right?

The Backend Processes

For all your backend things, I recommend a very simple checklist.

This can include items such as adding them to your programming software, making their program, adding them to any softwares that you use, updating their notes, for the team.

Whatever all the *"little things"* you do, task-wise, when you sign up a client... add that to an onboarding checklist.

After their First Visit

At this point, the client comes in for a day one workout and hopefully has a great experience. I would suggest that you immediately follow up with this first visit with a personal phone call. After a first visit, there are any number of things that could pop up, or questions that they might have but do not know who to ask.

Are they sore? Do they have questions on how to use the app or how to get into the Facebook group? This is the time to overcome any initial hesitations.

Send them an Automated Campaign Email

The final component to think about with onboarding is going to be the campaign that you're going to send them. Now, before we get too deep in this step, I want to ensure you understand the importance of the previous steps. Email marketing is great, but there are a lot of emails that get lost in spam folders, so you really need to get those personal touches [the phone call, the thank you cards and other mail offerings] right!

Ok, so for your email campaign that you send this new customer, I recommend that you build out a campaign that lasts for about 3-4 weeks and includes 2-3 emails per week. The e-mails should cover how they best utilize the features of their membership.

I would send an email on how they can schedule their appointments and anything that they need to know about your schedule policy. I might also add an email about how they get the most out of your client-only Facebook group. What about an email on what to do when they get injured or when they travel?

You'll notice that I didn't say anything about fitness tips or nutrition tips.

Although they may care about fitness tips and nutrition, it's more important for you and your business that they understand the basic ins and outs of membership, especially for the first thirty days after they joined. They need to feel a part of the community.

We can get them to fix their negative nutrition habits in month two.

Developing a Reward & Recognition System for Member Loyalty

Keeping members for a long time is the goal, but how exactly do you accomplish that? Of course, you want to ensure they are having a great experience and are getting great results.

However, what I have found to be just as impactful is to build in a reward and a recognition system. This isn't just one thing you do, it can be as big or as small as you'd like, but the key is that you do something. We know through behavioral psychology that if we want a behavior to repeat we need to reward it. We also know that people love being recognized, both individually, and publicly. A strong reward and recognition aims to hit all aspects of that.

Let's break this down into sections of the client journey...

Benefits to Joining your Gym

The first part of recognition and rewards is when a client first joins. That's a huge win, right? So we want to recognize that.

I like giving my clients a welcome bag with information about my program (need to know), a gift card or 7-day pass to give a friend or family member, and a sticker or water bottle.

In addition to the welcome bag, I like to mail a handwritten thank you note welcoming them to the family and showing my gratitude and excitement.

This is a great way to prevent buyer remorse and stand out in the marketplace, as no one else is doing that.

Celebrate Their Achievements

Once a client finishes their first workout, I recommend having a moment of celebration. At my gym, we pulled our t-shirt from our welcome bag and gave it to them after the first workout to make that a moment of recognition.

You also want to recognize the various milestones that they hit as they continue in their fitness journey. That can include six months, one year and two-year anniversaries.

The simple thing I recommend is a handwritten thank you note from you and the team congratulating them on the anniversary and reminding them of all the progress they have made.

It's important to take the time to recognize and reward them for those big items.

However, what about the wins each and every month? We don't want to let a month go by without them feeling like they are recognized and rewarded.

There are two key systems I recommend you install for this:

1. The Frequent Sweaters Club: This club celebrates everyone that shows up to the gym at least 10 times in the month. I recommend making a big chalkboard (just use chalkboard paint) that has everyone's name on it. Post the picture, tag everyone, and make a big deal of it every single month. You will be surprised how many people look forward to seeing their friends and others on the board.

The goal is to drive the motivation each month to just get your name on the board. Why? No one cancels their membership if they walked into your gym 10x this month.

2. **The *"Weekly Wins"* rhythm.**

This is a simple collection of client wins that gets emailed out and posted every Friday as a way to celebrate client wins that happened through the week.

So combine the lifetime recognition of celebrating clients hitting certain milestones and anniversaries combined with the monthly recognition of hitting attendance markers and weekly wins and you have a solid rewards and recognition system in place. This will not only increase member loyalty, but clients will be raving and want to refer their friends, growing your business.

Key Takeaways:

1. ***Streamline Onboarding****: Simplify your onboarding process to eliminate barriers for new clients. Make the first steps seamless and welcoming to reduce anxiety and improve retention.*

2. ***Celebrate Wins Regularly****: Implement systems to recognize client milestones, such as anniversaries and consistent attendance. Recognition builds loyalty and keeps members motivated.*

3. ***Personalize Communication****: Follow up with personal touches like handwritten notes and phone calls. These small efforts create a big impact on retention.*

PART V

Scale

Growing Your Business & Your Wealth

Chapter 17

Scaling Without Sacrificing Quality

The Blueprint for Growing Your Gym the Right Way

Here's the truth: growth is great, but if you're not careful, scaling can lead to a drop in quality. And when the quality slips, clients notice.

The best gyms grow without sacrificing the things that make them great. They build systems, train teams, and scale intentionally. That's how you maintain, or even improve, the client experience as you grow.Let's dive into how you can scale your gym while keeping the quality high.

Know What Makes Your Gym Special

Before you even think about scaling, you need to know what makes your gym unique.

Why do clients choose you? Why do they stay? Whatever it is, you need to fully commit to it. When you scale, those core differentiators need to stay intact.

Scaling isn't about diluting things to appeal to a bigger audience. It's about figuring out how to replicate what works. Talk to your best clients, dig into feedback, and identify the key aspects of your experience that must stay consistent as you grow. That's where you start.

Build Systems That Protect Quality

You've probably got a good handle on what works for your gym right now. But when it's time to grow, what worked on a small scale won't necessarily work as you expand. That's where systems come in. Scaling successfully requires you to systemize virtually every area of your business. That way, no matter how big you grow, your client experience stays consistent.

Let's break down some examples:

- **Onboarding**: How do you welcome new clients into your gym? Automate the paperwork, sure. But also create a standardized process that includes personal touchpoints to ensure the client gets the experience you want them to have.

- **Program Design**: As your client base grows, you'll need systems in place to ensure that your programming stays at the same high-quality. Whether it's small group training or individualized programs, you need to streamline and systemize the ability to deliver consistent, results-driven sessions.

- **Coaching Standards**: The more you scale, the less involved you'll be in every session. That's why it's crucial to have **clear session standards** for your coaches.

When you have systems like these in place, you're not just relying on memory or hope to maintain quality. You're building an infrastructure that ensures consistency as you grow.

Focus on Training Your Team

One of the biggest challenges when scaling is maintaining consistency across a larger team. When it's just you and a coach or two, it's easy to ensure everyone's on the same page. But as you add more staff, it becomes harder to keep everyone aligned with your standards and culture. That's why team development is so important.

First, hire the right people.

Look for coaches who don't just have the right resume, but also align with your gym's values and culture. Once you've got the right people on board, invest in ongoing training. Your team should be constantly learning and improving. Create a team onboarding program for new hires and build regular education into your operations. Whether it's through weekly team meetings or outside education, the more you invest in your team, the better your gym will be.

Automate Where It Makes Sense, But Keep It Personal

I know we've already talked about the importance of automation, but we are going to cover this again because it is *that* vital to scaling your business properly. Automation can streamline repetitive tasks and free up your time. But it should never replace the personal touch that belongs in personal training. So how do you strike the right balance? Automate the back-end tasks that don't directly impact the client experience:

- Scheduling emails and text reminders.

- Billing and payment processing.

- Outbound client check-ins and follow-up notifications that you engage in when there's a response.

These tasks can all be handled by automation, allowing you and your team to focus on what matters most – delivering an exceptional client experience. Remember, your clients come to your gym for a reason, and no automation can replace that.

Keep Your Eyes On Retention

As you grow, it's important to track the right metrics to ensure that quality remains high. While we cover numbers in detail in a different section of the book, the client retention rate will serve as your barometer in knowing if client experience might be slipping.

Stay Connected

As your gym grows, it's easy to go from being on the floor for most of the sessions to being absent from the clients' view as you get caught up in the business side of things. But if you want to maintain quality, you need to stay connected, often transitioning to the role of 'mayor' of the gym. When you stay connected, you'll ensure that the culture and quality of your gym remain strong as you scale. At the end of the day, scaling is about growing with intention – building systems, training your team, and staying connected to your mission. When you focus on maintaining quality at every step, you'll be able to grow without losing what makes your gym truly great.

Opening Additional Locations or Franchising: Scaling Your Gym Without Losing Control

Expanding your gym by opening additional locations or franchising can be appealing.

It can be a big and exciting step. But here's the reality: growth comes with challenges. And if you're not careful, you can easily lose the things that made your gym successful in the first place. But it doesn't have to go that way. With the right systems, people, and mindset, you can scale your gym while maintaining the same high standards that got you here.

Whether you're thinking about opening new locations or exploring franchising, the key is doing it strategically.

Know Where You Stand

Before you jump into expansion, take a good look at where your current gym is at.

A strong initial location is the foundation for any approach to scaling.

If your gym isn't running smoothly or consistently profitable, adding more locations won't fix that, it'll magnify the issues.

Start by asking yourself:

- Is my gym profitable and stable on its own?

- Are my systems solid enough to be replicated, or do we still need to iron out some details?

- Do I have the financial resources to fund this expansion?

Opening another gym or starting a franchise adds layers of complexity. You'll be managing a bigger team, more expenses, and more clients. If things aren't running like a well-oiled machine at your first location, expansion can sink everything instead of becoming your success story.

Build Systems That Work

One of the biggest challenges with scaling is that you can't be everywhere at once. And that's why systems are so crucial. You need systems that can replicate the experience and service your clients expect—even when your current team isn't the group delivering everything.

Think about things like:

- **Client acquisition:** How do you bring in clients, month after month?

- **Client onboarding**: How do you make clients feel welcome and supported from day one? Your new locations need to follow the same process.

- **Program consistency**: You want every client to have the same high-quality experience. Your programming should be standardized and easy to replicate.

- **Coaching standards**: It's critical to have clear coaching standards. Make sure your team knows what's expected and give them the tools to succeed.

Having these systems in place ensures that each location, whether it's owned by you or a franchisee, runs smoothly and consistently.

The Right People

Scaling isn't just about adding more locations. It's about finding the right people to help you run those locations, whether it's your team or franchisees. You'll need leaders who share your vision and understand your brand. These leaders need to be more than just employees, they should be team members who can uphold your gym's mission and maintain the culture you've worked hard to build. If you're franchising, it's even more important to find the right people. A franchisee is someone who will carry your brand forward in a whole new market. They need to have the passion and skills to represent your gym's values, and you need to have a strong franchisee training program in place to help them succeed.

Protect Your Brand

As you expand, remember that you're not just growing your business...you're expanding your brand. And with every new location, there's a chance your brand could lose its identity if you're not careful.Develop clear brand guidelines. Your brand is more than a logo or name, it's how your gym looks, feels, and interacts with clients. Every new location should follow the same guidelines to ensure consistency.

Franchising vs. Opening New Locations

There's a big difference between opening more gyms yourself and franchising your business.

- **Opening additional locations** means you'll have full ownership and control, but it also means you're responsible for the day-to-day operations of each location.

- **Franchising** allows you to grow in a different format because you're licensing your brand to other entrepreneurs. While this means less operational responsibility, it requires you to create a strong franchise model and ongoing support for your franchisees.

Both models can work, but the one you choose depends on your goals and how involved you want to be in running multiple locations.

Scaling with Intention

The excitement of growing your business can easily lead to getting in a hurry. But successful expansion isn't about how fast you grow, it's about how well you scale. Start small. If you're opening new locations, don't jump into three or four at once. Open one, make sure it's running smoothly, then scale up from there.

Maintain the standard for quality and client care that you've already established at your original location. Growth is only valuable if you can sustain it. Don't compromise on quality just to grow faster. Expanding beyond a single location is a big step, but it can be one of the best moves you make for your business. With the right systems, the right people, and a solid plan, you can scale your business without losing the quality and personal touch that made you successful in the first place.

Key Takeaways:

1. **Systemize Everything**: *Build replicable systems for onboarding, coaching, and client engagement to maintain quality as you grow. Your success depends on consistent experiences across locations.*

2. **Invest in Training**: *Develop your team with ongoing education to uphold your standards. Scaling requires leaders who align with your vision and values.*

3. **Expand Intentionally**: *Don't rush into new locations. Perfect your first gym's operations before replicating its success*

Chapter 18

Wealth Building for Gym Owners

Managing Gym Finances with the Profit First System

One of the biggest challenges gym owners face is managing their finances in a way that ensures both growth and profitability. Many gym owners find themselves struggling with cash flow, unexpected expenses, and slim profit margins. *The "Profit First"* system, popularized by Mike Michalowicz, has become a game-changer for small business owners, and the adaptation by John Briggs in *"Profit First for Microgyms"* provides specific strategies tailored for the fitness industry.

This chapter will break down how gym owners can use the Profit First system to take control of their finances and create a profitable business model.

1. Understanding the Profit First System

The general premise of Profit First is to treat *"profit"* as an expense. The traditional accounting formula for businesses is:

Sales - Expenses = Profit

In this formula, profit comes last, meaning most gym owners only take what's left after covering all their expenses—which often isn't much. The Profit First system flips this script, changing the formula to:

Sales - Profit = Expenses

With this mindset, profit becomes a priority. By allocating profit first and living within the remaining budget for expenses, gym owners can ensure their business remains financially healthy from the start.

2. The Core Accounts Structure

To implement Profit First effectively, you need to set up multiple bank accounts with distinct purposes. These accounts act as buckets for allocating funds as soon as revenue comes in. Now, don't let this overwhelm you. It's quite simple to set up accounts at your bank. The key is to set up multiple accounts so that your accounts look "smaller," thus you make wiser spending decisions. Michalowicz' book recommends more, but to simplify I recommend the following accounts.

Income Account: This is where all revenue from gym memberships, personal training, retail sales, and other sources initially lands. This is a holding account and funds will be dispersed from here into the other accounts. This is where all expenses come out, except the following:

Payroll Account: I recommend a separate account just for your payroll expense, as this expense is a gym's largest expense and grows over time.

Profit Account: A percentage of your revenue is immediately allocated here. This money is set aside as pure profit, and it's not to be touched for regular expenses. The goal is to accumulate profit steadily and use this account to reward yourself as the owner or reinvest in the business when needed.

Tax Account: One of the most painful surprises for business owners is the end-of-year tax bill. The Profit First system helps you plan by allocating a percentage of your revenue into a tax account, so when tax season comes around, you're fully prepared.

3. Setting Your Allocation Percentages

The magic of Profit First lies in the consistent allocation of funds based on your gym's revenue.

Here's a rough guide to start with your percentage allocations based on gross revenues:

- Income Account: 30%

- Payroll: 40%

- Profit Account: 20%

- Tax Account: 10%

These percentages may vary based on your gym's size, location, and financial situation, but the key is to start with a system and adjust over time.

If you're currently in a place where operating expenses are consuming most of your revenue, you'll need to slowly shift these percentages as you reduce expenses or increase revenue.

4. Cutting Unnecessary Expenses

One of the insights gym owners gain from the Profit First system is how much of their revenue is being eaten up by unnecessary expenses. Because your operating expenses account is only funded with a portion of your revenue, you're forced to examine where your money is going. Many gyms overspend on things like underutilized equipment, or advertising campaigns that don't yield a return on investment. The Profit First system compels you to streamline your expenses, so you only spend money on what directly impacts member growth and retention. I recommend you track your expenses each month, list out your expenses *before* the month starts in a **Monthly Spending Plan**. This allows you to see the expenses before they happen and make any necessary cuts.

5. Pay Yourself Consistently

One of the main reasons many gym owners burn out is that they don't pay themselves regularly. They pour their revenue back into the business, hoping it will eventually pay off, only to find themselves struggling to make ends meet personally. With the Profit First system, the profit account guarantees that you are compensated for your hard work. By making yourself a priority, you not only improve your personal financial situation, but you also create a sustainable business model that doesn't rely on sacrifice and burnout. As your gym grows, you can increase your pay rate over time by adjusting your allocation percentages.

The ultimate goal of the Profit First system is to build a financially healthy and profitable gym. By consistently allocating a portion of your revenue to profit, you'll begin to accumulate reserves that provide stability.

Start with small steps.

You don't need to achieve perfect allocation percentages overnight. Gradually implement the system, and as your gym becomes more profitable, you'll be able to allocate more toward profit and owner's pay.

Managing your gym's finances with the Profit First system helps ensure that your business isn't just surviving—it's thriving.

By flipping the traditional formula and putting profit first, you'll gain control over your finances, reduce unnecessary expenses, and build a business that rewards both you and your members. As you implement this system, remember that consistency is key. Over time, you'll create a financially healthy gym that supports both growth and long-term success.

Key Takeaways:

1. ***Put Profit First****: Adopt the "Profit First" system by allocating revenue to profit before covering expenses. This ensures a financially healthy and sustainable business.*

2. ***Diversify with Real Estate****: Invest in assets like gym buildings or short-term rentals. Real estate offers long-term wealth-building opportunities alongside your gym.*

3. ***Plan for Expansion Carefully****: Build a second location only when your first gym runs like a well-oiled machine. Strong foundations make scaling profitable.*

Chapter 19

Build a Wealth-Building Game Plan for Gym Owners

As a gym owner, your primary goal is likely to run a successful gym that provides exceptional value to your members. But beyond that, there's an opportunity to leverage your business to create long-term wealth. At Wealthy Gym Owner, we emphasize that making a healthy profit from your gym isn't just the end game—it's the beginning of a wealth-building journey. In this chapter, I'll outline how you can craft a wealth-building game plan that turns your business into a vehicle for lasting financial security and freedom. I chose to do this through investing in real estate, specifically Short Term Rentals (vacation rentals), but that is not the only path.

1. Profit as the Foundation for Wealth

The first step in building wealth is ensuring that your gym is consistently profitable. You can't begin planning for long-term wealth without first making sure your business generates a steady, healthy profit. This involves creating a solid financial system, using the Profit First model, that ensures you are prioritizing profit and controlling expenses. Once your gym is profitable, it's essential to look at how you're using that profit.Rather than letting extra revenue sit in a bank account or reinvesting all of it back into your gym, you should allocate a portion of it to wealth-building strategies that extend beyond your business [be patient, we'll dive into these strategies in a moment]. This shift in mindset—from simply growing the gym to using the gym to grow your personal wealth—is the foundation of your wealth-building game plan.

2. Establishing Your Financial Goals

Before diving into specific wealth-building strategies, it's important to clearly define your financial goals.

Do you want to generate passive income streams outside of your gym, or are you looking for a more active investment?

Start by setting both short-term and long-term goals. Short-term goals might include reaching a certain income milestone or paying off business debt, while long-term goals could involve investing in real estate, opening multiple gym locations, or building a retirement portfolio. By defining your goals, you'll be able to create a roadmap for how to get there. Your wealth-building plan should be aligned with the life you envision for yourself—whether that's financial independence, more flexibility in your daily schedule, or even scaling down your involvement in the business while still benefiting from its success.

3. Diversifying Income Streams

A key element in building long-term wealth is diversifying your income streams beyond your gym. While a successful gym can be a great business, relying solely on one source of income limits your ability to build true financial security.

Important Note: I don't recommend diversifying until you have maximized your first location. It can be easy to jump to the next thing or to try a passive income strategy, but this is a distraction. Your best opportunity is growing your first location.

Once that is fully optimized and at capacity, there are several ways gym owners can diversify their income:

- **Real Estate Investment:** One of the most effective ways to build wealth is through real estate. You can start by investing in short-term rentals (STRs), long-term rentals, or even purchasing the building your gym operates in. Real estate not only generates passive income but also builds equity over time, providing long-term value. If you're looking at buying the building your gym operates in, I would highly recommend you check out the SBA 504 program.

- **Scaling to Multiple Locations:** If your gym is profitable and your systems are dialed in, you may want to consider opening additional locations.

With the right management in place, having multiple gyms can create multiple revenue streams, resulting in a scaled your business that increases your earning potential. Now, I have two key points I want to stress with this option:

1. Your first location has to be running like a well-oiled machine.

2. You have to desire managing and leading people, as that will become your primary role.

4. Developing a Wealth-Building Game Plan

Now that you've identified potential income streams, it's time to create a detailed plan to implement these strategies. This plan should map out specific actions, timelines, and targets to keep you on track.

- **Step 1: Maximize Your Gym's Profitability:** Ensure your gym is consistently profitable before moving into other ventures. Tighten up your operations, manage expenses, and create sustainable revenue streams from memberships, personal training, and retail sales. Your gym should act as the financial engine that fuels your wealth-building activities.

- **Step 2: Allocate Profit for Investment:** Once your gym is generating healthy profits, allocate a percentage of that income specifically for wealth-building activities. Set up a separate investment account and decide on a percentage—5%, 10%, or more—to contribute regularly. This consistent investment will compound over time.

- **Step 3: Choose Your First Wealth-Building Venture:** Decide which wealth-building strategy aligns best with your goals. If real estate appeals to you, start with a small investment, such as purchasing a rental property or STR. If opening multiple gyms is your focus, begin planning for your second location. The key is to choose one venture to focus on initially before branching out further.

- **Step 4: Automate and Delegate:** As you diversify your income streams, avoid becoming overwhelmed by trying to do everything yourself. Invest in automation, hire capable team members, and outsource tasks where necessary. The goal of your wealth-building plan is not to create more work for yourself but to set up passive or semi-passive income streams that run without your constant oversight.

5. Review and Adjust Regularly

Your wealth-building game plan isn't static.

As your gym grows and your financial situation evolves, you'll need to regularly review and adjust your strategy. Set aside time every quarter to evaluate your progress, adjust your allocation percentages, and explore new opportunities for growth.

Building a wealth-building game plan as a gym owner requires intention, strategy, and long-term thinking. By focusing on profitability, diversifying your income streams, and allocating your profits wisely, you can create a financial future that extends beyond the walls of your gym. Whether through real estate, scaling your gym operations, or exploring other ventures, your gym can be the foundation for lasting wealth and financial independence.

Key Takeaways:

1. **Set Clear Financial Goals:** *Define short- and long-term wealth goals to guide your investments. Align your plan with your vision for financial independence and flexibility.*

2. **Allocate for Investments:** *Use gym profits to fund income streams like real estate or additional locations. Reinvent revenue to grow wealth outside of your primary business.*

3. **Develop Exit Strategies:** *Whether selling or franchising, create a game plan that ensures your gym remains valuable and attractive to future buyers.*

Chapter 20

Preparing For The Future

Exits & Expansions

As a gym owner, it's essential to think beyond the day-to-day operations of your business and plan for the future. Whether you're considering expanding to multiple locations, diversifying your offerings, or ultimately exiting the business, strategic planning is key to long-term success. In this chapter, we'll explore how to create a future-focused plan that prepares your gym for growth, scale, and eventual exit, ensuring that you maximize your returns and continue to build wealth.

1. Define Your Long-Term Vision

Before diving into specifics about expansions or exits, the first step is to define your long-term vision. Ok, I know we've talked about your vision for your gym quite a lot, but that's because it's really important. Here we are focusing on your long-term vision for your gym. Ask yourself honestly, Where do you see your gym in five, ten, or even twenty years? Do you want to scale to multiple locations, focus on a premium single-location experience, or eventually sell the business?

To be clear, your goals do not need to be perfect or set in stone, but having a sense of general direction is important.

Unsure about your Long-term Vision?

Having a clear vision of where you want to go will influence every decision you make moving forward. If you're unsure, consider the following questions:

- Do you want to be deeply involved in the day-to-day operations, or do you prefer to take a more hands-off approach over time?

- Are you driven by the idea of growing and scaling your business, or is financial security, through a single profitable location more appealing?

- What role do you want your gym to play in your overall wealth-building strategy?

Once you have a clear vision, you can create a strategic plan that aligns with your goals, whether it's preparing for an expansion or setting up for a future exit.

2. Expanding Your Business: A Growth Strategy

Expanding your gym—whether through opening new locations, adding new services, or targeting new markets—can be a highly profitable move, but it requires careful planning. Here are key factors to consider when planning for expansion:

- **Systematize Your Operations** - Before expanding, you need
  to ensure that your current location operates like a well-oiled
  machine. Can your gym run smoothly without your constant
  presence? If not, you may need to focus on building systems and
  processes that allow your gym to be self-sustaining.

- Standardized operations—from sales and marketing to customer
  service and member retention—will make it easier to replicate
  success when you expand. Consider creating a detailed operation
  (digital) manual that outlines every key process in your gym. This
  not only allows your current gym to thrive, but also serves as a
  roadmap for future locations.

- **Assess the Market** - Expanding into new locations or markets
  requires thorough research.Conduct a market analysis to identify
  areas with high demand for your services but low competition.
  Look at factors such as population demographics, local fitness
  trends, and proximity to other gyms. The goal is to find areas
  where your gym can thrive without immediately facing market
  saturation.

- Also, consider the financial aspects of expansion. How much
  capital will you need to open a new location, and how long will
  it take for that location to become profitable? Make sure your
  existing gym is financially strong before taking on the risks of
  expansion.

- **Leverage Your Brand** - If you've built a strong brand and
  reputation with your current gym, leverage that when expanding.
  Branding consistency across locations builds member trust and

loyalty. Use the same marketing strategies, social media presence, and value propositions across all locations to ensure that your brand identity remains intact.

- **Build a Strong Team for Growth** - Your ability to expand successfully will heavily depend on having the right people in place. As you open new locations or add new services, you'll need managers, trainers, and staff who can operate independently and maintain the high standards you've set. Consider promoting from within your organization, offering leadership development opportunities for employees who show promise. Having a strong team in place will allow you to focus on the bigger picture, such as growing the business or looking into new markets.

3. Plan for an Exit

While expanding may be your immediate focus, it's equally important to consider your exit strategy. Whether you plan to sell the business, pass it down to a family member, or transition into a more passive ownership role, having a clear exit strategy ensures that you can maximize the value of your gym when the time comes.

When I sold my gym, here are some key lessons that I learned:

If you want to sell your gym one day, it needs to be attractive to potential buyers.

A sellable gym has a strong, loyal member base, healthy financials, and systems that allow it to run without the owner's constant involvement.

To prepare for a potential sale:

- **Increase profitability**: Buyers are interested in businesses that generate strong profits. Focus on maximizing revenue and controlling costs to improve your bottom line.

- **Create documented systems**: A gym with well-documented operations is easier to transfer to new owners. Have everything from staff training to member acquisition processes clearly laid out.

- **Develop a strong team**: Buyers will feel more confident if they know your staff is capable of running the gym without relying too much on you.

When planning an exit, it's crucial to understand how your gym will be valued.

Gyms are typically valued based on a multiple of their earnings before interest, taxes, depreciation, and amortization (EBITDA).

The healthier your profit margins, the higher the multiple you can command.

Make sure to have your financial records in order, including clean balance sheets, detailed profit-and-loss statements, and a track record of strong cash flow. If selling is your ultimate goal, consider bringing in a business valuation expert to help determine the current value of your gym and what steps you can take to increase its worth. There are several exit options, and it's important to choose the one that aligns with your personal and financial goals:

- **Selling the business outright**: This provides a lump sum, allowing you to cash out and move on to other ventures.

- **Partnering with an employee**: If you want to remain involved in the business but reduce your role, you can bring in a partner to take over part of the ownership while you retain a portion of equity. This may be suitable for a long-time employee who is your day-to-day manager, but tread lightly here.

4. Balancing Expansion and Exit Goals

Some gym owners may want to grow their business through expansions while also planning for an eventual exit.

These two goals are not mutually exclusive. Successful expansions can increase the value of your gym and make it more attractive to potential buyers. The key is to maintain focus on both goals and ensure that your expansion plans are aligned with your long-term exit strategy. As you expand, continue to build your gym's brand, profitability, and systems in a way that will make it easier to sell or transition down the road. Expanding with the right foundation in place will not only grow your business, but also maximize its value when you're ready to move on. Planning for the future of your gym—whether through expansions, new services, or an eventual exit—requires strategic thinking and intentional action. By systematizing your operations, building a strong brand, and keeping an eye on your financial health, you can set your gym up for long-term success. Whether your goal is to grow and scale or to prepare for a profitable exit, having a future-focused game plan will ensure that your gym continues to thrive, allowing you to build wealth and financial freedom in the process.

Key Takeaways:

1. ***Think Beyond Day-to-Day****: Prepare your gym for potential exits*

or expansions by building a brand that thrives without you. Systems and a strong team are key.

2. ***Balance Growth with Exit Plans****: Use profitable expansions to increase your gym's value while planning an eventual transition. Strategic growth maximizes long-term rewards.*

3. ***Stay Future-Focused****: Align every decision with your long-term vision. Whether you scale, sell, or delegate, clarity and preparation ensure success.*

Chapter 21

Conclusion

The Wealthy Gym Owner Path

Becoming a wealthy gym owner is not just about financial success; it's about building a sustainable business that supports your lifestyle, serves your clients, and grows consistently. Over the course of this book, we've laid out a path filled with actionable strategies, smart systems, and a mindset shift that moves you from being a trainer to a business owner. Now, let's recap some of the key strategies that can help you craft your own success story as a gym owner and ensure you stay motivated while avoiding burnout.

Recap of Key Strategies

Vision and Goals - Every journey begins with a vision. Crafting a clear vision of what your gym should look like sets the foundation for success. It's not just about the physical space but also the atmosphere, culture, and values. From this vision, break down actionable goals that serve as stepping stones toward achieving your half-million-dollar gym. These goals must be **specific, measurable, and time-bound** to track your progress.

Shifting from Trainer to Business Owner - One of the most significant changes for gym owners is moving from the role of a hands-on trainer to that of a CEO. It requires a mindset shift where you delegate tasks, build systems, and focus on long-term growth rather than day-to-day operations. This allows you to scale your business and avoid being trapped in a never-ending cycle of client sessions and operational stress.

Systems for Consistency - Systems are the backbone of any successful business. Whether it's onboarding clients, running marketing campaigns, or managing finances, creating **scalable systems** ensures consistency and allows your gym to operate smoothly even when you're not there. A well-run gym isn't dependent on the owner being involved in every detail—systems make this possible.

Client Retention Over Acquisition - While bringing in new clients is important, keeping the clients you already have is where long-term profit lies. Focus on creating systems for client engagement, regular check-ins, and special events to build a community within your gym. Remember, a client who stays with you for years is far more valuable than one who leaves after a few months. **Retention is key** to sustainable growth.

Marketing Mastery - Marketing is the lifeblood of a thriving gym, but it doesn't have to be complex. Develop a marketing calendar that includes **lead generation, client engagement, and referral campaigns**.

Use automation to keep the marketing machine running smoothly and incorporate both organic strategies and paid ads. Referral marketing is particularly powerful, allowing your existing clients to bring in new business while you focus on delivering great results.

Pricing for Profitability - Setting the right pricing structure is crucial to running a profitable gym. Rather than competing on price, focus on the value you deliver. Design membership tiers that cater to different client needs, ensuring you have a model that encourages long-term commitment and recurring revenue. Your pricing should reflect the transformation you offer, not just the sessions you provide.

Crafting Your Own Gym Owner Success Story

Now, it's time to craft your own success story. Whether you're just starting or have been in business for a while, the strategies in this book are your roadmap. Here's how to start building your success story today:

Refine Your Vision - If you haven't already, sit down and take time to clearly define the long-term vision for your gym. What do you want it to become? How will it serve your clients? What impact will it have on your community? A powerful vision guides every decision you make and keeps you motivated during tough times.

Set Actionable Goals - Break down your vision into concrete, actionable goals. Whether it's reaching a certain revenue target, bringing in a specific number of clients, or launching new services, each goal should align with your broader vision. Make sure to review and adjust these goals regularly to stay on track.

Delegate and Build a Team - You can't do it all. One of the best things you can do to grow your business is to trust others. Invest in hiring, training, and developing a team that supports your vision. Your role is to lead and strategize, not micromanage every session. Trust your trainers and staff to execute the systems you've put in place.

Master the Art of Retention - Retention is your most powerful growth tool. Build deep relationships with your clients, personalize their experiences, and celebrate their successes. Creating a community where your clients feel valued and supported will not only keep them around, but also turn them into advocates for your gym.

Embrace Continuous Improvement - Success is never final. Continually refine your systems, marketing strategies, and client experience. Commit to learning and growing, both personally and professionally. Regularly assess what's working and what needs adjustment to keep your gym on the path to success.

Final Thoughts on Maintaining Momentum and Avoiding Burnout

Building a successful gym is a marathon, not a sprint. It requires commitment, strategy, and a clear focus on the long-term picture. But along the way, it's easy to get overwhelmed, especially as your responsibilities grow. Here are some strategies to help you maintain momentum and avoid burnout:

- **Prioritize Self-Care** - As much as you care for your clients, you need to care for yourself. Schedule time for your own fitness, mental health, and relaxation. Taking care of your body and mind ensures that you're able to lead your business effectively. Remember, you can't pour from an empty cup.

- **Delegate Wisely** - You don't have to do everything yourself. Delegate tasks that drain your energy and focus on high-impact activities that move your business forward. Trust your team to handle day-to-day operations so you can focus on growth, strategy, and leadership.

- **Celebrate Milestones-** It's easy to get caught up in the hustle and forget to celebrate your wins. Take time to recognize both small and large achievements, whether it's hitting a revenue goal, launching a new program, or receiving positive client feedback. Celebrating milestones keeps you motivated and reinforces the progress you're making.

- **Stay Focused on Your *'Why'* -** During challenging times, reconnect with the reason you started your gym in the first place. Whether it was to help people transform their lives or to create financial freedom for yourself, staying connected to your 'why' will help you push through the inevitable hurdles and keep you grounded.

The wealthy gym owner path isn't just about achieving financial success; it's about building a business that enhances your life and the lives of your clients.

By focusing on vision, systems, retention, and personal growth, you can create a gym that not only hits revenue goals but also stands the test of time. Now, it's up to you to take the knowledge from this book and build the future you've envisioned.

We Want To GIFT You Over $315 Worth Of Wealthy Gym Owner Resources... FOR FREE!

Are you ready to finally take your business to the next level? We'll give you Instant Access to this Wealth Building Collection...

Wealth-Building Workshop ($99 Value): Turn your gym into a cash-flow engine that generates wealth today and secures your future.

Fitness CEO Workshop ($99 Value): Step confidently into the CEO role and focus on strategic growth.

Hiring Workshop($79 Value): Build a team that aligns with your vision and helps your gym thrive.

Gym Growth Calculator ($39 Value): Unlock Your Gym's Potential Today! Ready to see your gym's capacity and growth potential? This calculator takes the guesswork out of growing your facility.

All You Have To Do Is Fill In The Form At WealthyGymGift.com, And Instant Access To This Wealthy Building Gift Collection Is Yours... For FREE!

Go To WealthyGymGift.com Now!

About the Authors

Doug Spurling

With over 15 years of experience in the fitness industry, Doug Spurling has established himself as a respected figure in fitness entrepreneurship and wealth creation.

As the founder of a highly successful training gym for 12 years, he developed expertise in leadership, client experience, and business operations. His dedication and strategic vision not only led to the gym's success but also resulted in a lucrative sale, fetching over seven figures.

Using the cash flow from his gym, Doug ventured into Short Term Rental real estate investment, where he skillfully built a portfolio now valued at over $14 million. He continues to add to that portfolio to create generational wealth for his family.

Doug shares his knowledge and insights with fellow gym owners as a coach and mentor. He helps them systemize and scale their fitness businesses, enabling them to find their ideal roles within their gyms while also building wealth outside of them.

Beyond his professional pursuits, Doug has a beautiful wife and four crazy kids who keep him on his toes. Balancing the hustle with family time ain't always easy, but it's what keeps him grounded and hungry for more.

Pat Rigsby

Pat Rigsby is a dad, husband, business coach, author, and entrepreneur who has built over 35 different businesses, including two Entrepreneur Franchise 500 award-winning franchises.

After a successful career as a college baseball coach, he got his entrepreneurial start by opening a personal training business and health club. Over the next few years, his small personal training business grew to a network of successful businesses ranging from franchises and certification companies to info-marketing and coaching and consulting.

He's shared his journey onstage in front of thousands, and has been featured in Entrepreneur, Men's Health, USA Today, and hundreds of other media outlets as well as authoring or co-authoring 20 books. For Pat, the best part is that he's been able to do all this while working from home, coaching his kids' sports teams, and enjoying a type of entrepreneurial lifestyle he never would have thought possible just a few years ago.

Made in the USA
Monee, IL
29 January 2025

11219695R00098